CONTEN

ACKNOWLEDGEMENTS

Behind every workaholic actor/writer/filmmaker is a team of cheerleaders, and I am lucky enough to have my amazing team...

My partner, James Pinkerton. Without him I would never have turned this book around within ten months. Thank you for always believing in me and supporting this book from when it was a mere thought. I am extremely lucky to have you in my life and love you lots.

To my parents, Anil, Jill and Steve. Thank you for loving and supporting me from the beginning. Not once have I ever heard anything but encouragement and pride when it comes to my career. You fuel the fire that keeps me going every day.

To my sisters, Suki and Karis. You are my everything. Life has never felt empty because you both are in it.

Thank you Ali Afzal, Chloë Adlerstein, Ieva Umbraiste and Jamie Hunt for your wonderful feedback and support. My accountability partner Julia Van Geldern for keeping me hitting those deadlines every week. Last but not least, Rosie Walton and the team at Book Printing UK for making the whole publishing process feel so easy.

I would like to dedicate this book to my nieces, nephews and little cousins: Ava, Eden, Evie, Mia, Leo, Theo, Ashton, Harley, Oliver, Leo, Oceano, Maurice, Arya, Alexander, Kai, Sienna and Archie. Whatever you choose to do in life, may you find happiness and fulfilment and never be afraid to follow the things that you love.

Lastly, I would like to dedicate this book to you, the reader. Thank you for giving me the time to share with you all that I have learnt. I wish you all of the success that you deserve and one day I hope to share the screen with you.

ACTORPRENEUR

A Working Actor's Guide

BY JADE ASHA

ACTORPRENEUR
© 2020 JADE ASHA
All rights reserved

ISBN: 978-1-5272-7734-2

ABOUT THE AUTHOR

Jade is an award winning Mauritian/English Actor and Filmmaker. She was born in South London and lived there until her family relocated to Norwich in her teens. At the age of 17 she returned to London to begin her acting career which has spanned TV, film, theatre and voiceovers. Jade is best known for her role as Naeema in THE INTENT.

In 2009 due to lack of auditions, Jade began creating her own acting work and has never looked back. Jade is now CEO of London Independent Pictures and has produced award winning films which she has both written and performed in. She also runs a successful voiceover company Jade Asha Voiceovers.

www.londonindependentpictures.com
www.jadeashavoiceovers.com
www.actorpreneurbook.com

PREFACE

As an actor you can never do enough for your career. There is always another film to watch, show to see, course to do, event to attend, email to send or person to meet. Sometimes, it can be a little overwhelming.

Myself, I love a good book and judging by the impressive spilling out bookcases of my actor friends, so do they. When searching for a book on acting recently, I knew exactly what I wanted. I wanted a modern, easy-to-read, how-to book on the business of acting which incorporated social media and making your own work. I wanted it to be about the British industry, which I have learnt to love and battle with myself, and I wanted it written by someone who I could relate to, who had endured the same battles that I had.

Having been in the industry for over fifteen years, I often found myself giving advice to new actors, on set or in audition rooms. Strangers often message me on social media and LinkedIn asking advice for themselves, their friends or their children. Whether it's to do with getting an agent, working with an agent, producing films, finding photographers or social media, the list goes on.

I hear stories of actors getting ripped off all the time and it breaks my heart. I tell people all of the things I wish someone had told me when I first started out. Then it struck me. Perhaps if I was looking for this book, there would be other people looking for it too. I am not a teacher, nor do I profess to know everything, and I am still learning myself. This book has been written from pure personal experience and nothing else. If I have made any mistakes or misinterpreted anything then I apologise and do not mean to offend. For those more experienced actors, I hope you can find comfort in hearing from someone who has had similar experiences and understands what actors have to go through, in a career which can otherwise be quite lonely.

INTRODUCTION

The problem with acting is that your career is always in someone else's hands. First, it's whether you get into drama school or not. Then, it's whether an agent wants to represent you. Only, they won't represent you unless you have acting credits and you can't get acting credits without an agent. Then, say you get an agent, it's now down to the agent and whether they spend enough time submitting you for work. If they submit you for work, will the casting director call you in? If you get called in for an audition, will they give you the job? If you finally get a job, will your scene get cut or the production fall to pieces and your footage never see the light of day?

Sounds bleak, doesn't it? What if I were to tell you it doesn't have to be that way? You can be the architect of your own acting career. You shouldn't be waiting for the phone to ring, you should be making the calls yourself. If you are willing to do what it takes and put the work in, I can show you how to become a working actor. I can't promise you fame or fortune, but I can show you how to grow your credits and keep busy. You will have to be willing to be in this for the long run, and you have to be willing to step out of your comfort zone and learn new skills.

So, why should you listen to me? Well, they say everyone loves the underdog. I don't expect you to love me, but I am certainly the underdog. Firstly, I don't come from money and I don't come from any kind of acting or entertainment background. I first fell in love with acting at the age of 13 but I had admired actors and performers my entire life. I have been financially independent since the age of 16 and moved to London at the age of 17. At the same time as I gained my first acting credits, I was rejected from drama schools 30 times, over the space of four years. I was always told that the odds were against me. Each school would only take on one 'Indian' girl a year due to the lack of roles available to me in the industry. My ethnicity is mixed Mauritian and English.

Over the next fifteen years I learnt to write, edit and produce, I trained to be an advanced stage combat performer, and I set up my own film production company – London Independent Pictures – and voiceover company – Jade Asha Voiceovers. I've recorded over 700 voiceover jobs and have over 70 acting credits to my name which span film, television and theatre and I have won several awards for my work. Having produced and cast many of my own and other people's productions, I am blessed with having a casting director's perspective too. I have used Spotlight (the British casting directory) as an actor, an agent and a casting director, as well as running multiple casting sessions and booking many actors for jobs.

I studied film financing at the National Film and Television School where our tutor, a professional producer, taught all of his producer students the importance of having 'name' actors attached to their scripts. I have sat in multiple meetings with producers discussing the reasons they do and don't want to book actors. That's a whole lot of valuable and interesting information for an actor to have.

My methods are contemporary. I utilise technology in every way that I can and sometimes my approach is a little unorthodox. In this book I promise to share with you everything I have learnt and my approach to my career. I will cover subjects not traditionally written about in acting books including intimate scenes, dumping your agent, attending premieres, creating your own work and managing your own PR. Whatever stage you are at in your acting career, I hope that in this book you will find some kind of inspiration or guidance which you will be able to implement into your own career.

So, what are you waiting for? Are you really doing everything you can? Are you presenting yourself in the best light? Somewhere out there, there is a role perfect for you being cast right now. But how are you going to get cast if they don't know who you are? What more can you do?

Read on to find out…

CHAPTER 1

CONFIDENCE

One of the first and most important steps towards becoming an actor is being able to say out loud, 'I am an actor' and believe it. If you haven't been to a prestigious school, are not part of Equity, don't have professional acting film, theatre or television credits or have been out of work for a while, it is easy to feel undeserving of the title. Yet you live and breathe it.

When someone asks you, 'what is it you do?' do you respond with an uncomfortable mumble of, 'I'm sort of…I want to be…I'm sometimes…I used to be an actor.' Or do you proudly announce, a little louder than you should, 'I'm an actor!'

No matter what stage of your career you are at, you will know. If nothing comes close to that connection you feel when you breathe as another person, when you speak their thoughts, when you cry someone else's tears and you feel their pain, you are an actor and you need to give yourself permission to call yourself one. And no matter what hardships this career throws at you, no one can ever take this away from you.

NO OTHER CHOICE

So, this is one for the newbies who have made no big commitments yet and are still undecided on their career path. Do not become an actor unless you absolutely have no choice. It is categorically one of the most difficult careers there is. If you are looking for stability, a well-paid job, a clear pathway and career progression, I strongly suggest that you choose a different career. Anything really! Just not a career in acting or entertainment. However, if you can handle rejection, uncertainty, insecurity and a spontaneous, unstructured lifestyle, then this is the job for you. You need to be incredibly resilient and not too proud to have a side job to get you through the quiet times.

So, if all of that sounds great, you have come to the right place. If you have taken all of this into account and are still happy to proceed on this journey, then congratulations! Nice to meet you. You sound like you're a little bit bad ass and right up my street. We both agree there is absolutely no other possible path you would like to spend your life strutting down, and what an adventure it is. From the bottom of my heart I really hope you are one of the fortunate ones who lands dream job after dream job. For the other 85 per cent, or whatever the stats are, who spend most of their career 'resting', let's get started on a plan to make sure that you are always busy.

STEP OVER THE ROPE

We have established that you are an actor and that you definitely want to do this! Now we need to keep that confidence going and make sure it covers all areas of your life, including your performance. To start with, I want to tell you a little bit about a eureka moment I had at the Academy Drama School, a part-time foundation acting course that I did at the age of 18.

Our head teacher was an amazingly jolly man, but his methods were a little bizarre. One day he laid out a skipping rope in the middle of the dance studio floor. He asked us students to line up and one by one step over the rope, so we did. After we stepped, he would tell us if we had passed the test or had to try again.

The first person walked up to the rope, jumped over it, and then looked at him for approval. He said, 'no, get to the back of the line,' a cheeky twinkle in his eye. The next student walked up to the rope and stomped over it, wrinkling their face up, flirting for a yes. 'Nope, off you go.' It went on. One by one we jumped the rope and got rejected. We had no idea what we were doing wrong. The more we jumped, the more desperate we were for approval. Jumping in different ways, stepping, showing off, trying our best to please him. It was still a no. We had no idea what he wanted.

Finally, one of the oldest students stepped over very calmly. She got a yes. We couldn't figure out what she had done to get it right. Eventually, after ten minutes or more of jumping over that bloody rope we got bored and lost enthusiasm. Then, I stepped over the rope for the twentieth time. All of a sudden, he said, 'yes'. I had no idea what had changed. It slowly dawned on us that the less we cared about trying to do it right, the more yes's that came, until eventually we had all successfully stepped over the rope.

'Do you know why you got a yes?' he smirked. We couldn't figure it out! 'Because you stopped looking for approval. You were confident. You weren't worried about pleasing me. You stopped wanting that "yes". You simply stepped over the rope.'

Though I didn't know it then, it was one of the most important lessons of my career. Desperation can be very visible, especially for people who see it all day long. It's magnified even more so in front of a camera lens. Ever been rejected by someone that you fancy? Funny how the moment you lose interest, that person starts being interested in you. Could it be the same in acting? The more desperately you want the job, the less likely you are to get it. If you just concentrate on the task at hand, however – stop texting your crush, concentrate on the audition, step over the rope – that is where the confidence lies.

Concentrate on the work, stop trying to please people.

MANIFEST
Say you're going on holiday. You've packed your bags and booked

your time off work, but you haven't picked a destination and have no idea where you're going. You'll probably end up wasting a lot of valuable sun lounger time. When you go on holiday it's also very likely that you'll know what the weather is going to be like, if you need vaccinations to go there, where the accommodation is, the transfers, flight time, departure and arrival airport. If you're a foodie like me, you may even have planned which restaurants you will be eating in. So, why wouldn't you put the same kind of planning into your career?

I'm not saying you can choose what drama school, agent or casting director accepts you, but if know what you want, you should be able to figure out a way to get it. Say you want to be in musical theatre, it's better to invest in dancing and singing lessons than acting for camera classes. Or if action films are your calling, better to do martial arts and gymnastics than flute lessons. The point is, if we know our destination our wonderful human brain will figure out a way to get us there. Even subconsciously.

Now time for some homework. If you haven't done a vision board before, you're in for a treat. It is an incredibly powerfully tool and I am still shocked when I look back over the years that I've ended up living the life I once dreamed about in pictures. A vision board can simply be a collage of photos that represent the things that you want in life. My last one included publishing my first book, something that I never thought that I would do. Just saying.

Before you start on your vision board, I want you to take a moment to think about your ideal future you. Close your eyes and visualise it, if it helps. You are retired in 40 years' time. You wake up in your bed. What does it feel like? What does your bedroom look like? Take a deep breath in, what does it smell like? What is the temperature like? What country are you in? Get out of bed and walk around your house. What does the house look like? Walk around each room. Do you have pets? Is anyone else there? Do you have grandchildren? Are your children all grown up? Do you have a partner? Do you have a garden? Go outside and look at the house. Is it a big house? Small? Swimming pool? Horses in the back yard? Now, go back inside. You have a room. It's full of your lifetime achievements. Film and television posters with your face on them? Westend posters? Awards? For best actor? How many? Were you executive producer? Writer? Director, even? How many awards? Take a moment to take it all in. Now open your eyes.

To listen to a free guided audio version of this visualisation go to https://www.actorpreneurbook.com/guidedvisualisation

I hope you enjoyed that as much as I did the first time that I walked around my dream life. Now do the same again but this time imagine what your life looks like in thirty, ten, five, and one year's time. By now you might have a clearer picture of what your life goals are. Now it's time to put them on your vision board. You can do this using vision board apps, by saving images on Google and Pinterest, or, if you're a little more old school like me, then you can cut photos out of magazines and stick them to a large piece of paper. Whatever works for you. Have fun with it. Add holidays that you want to go on, what your health and wellness look like, how to spend your free time. Your imagination is the limit.

When this is complete, put it somewhere you can look at it every day. Print it and put it up on your wall or use it as a screensaver on your phone or computer. Now it's time to take action as we figure out how to get there.

CHAPTER 2

TRAINING AND DRAMA SCHOOLS

Before embarking in a career as an actor, I strongly recommend that you do drama training of some sort. This could be an after-school class, a weekend drama class, a college course or a beginner/foundation course in acting or performing arts. Here, you will learn the foundations and absolute basics that you need to know to work as an actor. This will include learning how to connect with your body, your voice, the text and how to warm up and warm down. You will also learn acting terminology and know how to put it into practice, for example, stage left, right, upstage, downstage, upstaging.

Most importantly, you will learn how to work with other actors and directors and begin to understand how to handle and adapt to different personalities, how to take direction and learn that it is not an actor's place to give it. You will find your strengths, as a performer and personally, and what you need to work on. It will give you a safe space to make mistakes, play and get creative. Most courses will include a performance at the end of each term. This will start building your all-important credits for your CV.

Eventually, you will need to join casting platforms such as Spotlight or Mandy.com. To apply for membership you will be required to have some professional credits or professional training. Though college performances are not seen as professional credits, they are better than no credits, especially when applying for acting jobs.

Breaking into the industry with only basic training is completely doable – I did it – but it can also be seen as the long way around. The more traditional path, and here I'm referring to drama schools, has no more guarantees of success but it can launch you in front of the eyes of Casting Directors (CDs) and agents.

DRAMA SCHOOLS

Drama school is not the be all and end all of an actor's career, but it certainly helps. Usually it includes three years of intense training from the top teachers, seminars with famous alumni and that dreamy industry showcase at the end. Becoming a student is no easy feat, and that is speaking from experience. I believe the top drama schools and universities still include the following:

Royal Academy of Dramatic Arts (Rada), London Academy of Music and Dramatic Arts (LAMDA), Bristol Old Vic Theatre School, Royal Conservatoire Of Scotland, ALRA, Royal Welsh College of Music and Drama, Oxford School of Drama, Central School of Speech and Drama, Guildhall School of Music and Drama, Italia Conti Academy of Theatre Arts, Mountview Academy of Theatre Arts, East 15 Acting School, Rose Brutford College of Theatre and Performance and Manchester Metropolitan.

These days you can expect to pay between £12- £80 per audition, so if you are applying to a few schools you can rack up a pretty hefty bill.

PROS AND CONS

Deciding if drama school is for you can be a difficult process and there is a lot to prepare and invest into the auditioning process itself. Drama School isn't for everyone. Here is a list of pros and cons to consider before applying:

Pros:
- Industry recognition
- Great connections
- Amazing experience

- BA HONs qualification (useful for finding alternative post-graduate jobs if you decide not to pursue acting)
- Drama School Showcase and introductions to agents and casting directors
- World-renowned training
- A vast range of skills
- Three years of solid acting experience and credits for your CV

Cons:

- Expensive
- Competitive
- No guarantees of work
- Potential relocation required
- Tough auditioning process
- Time consuming course
- Debt
- Unrealistic expectation of success after graduating

If you are looking for a career in the theatre, then I strongly recommend that you do try your chances at going to a drama school. Drama Schools were, after all, built to train theatre actors. If you are more inclined towards television and film, then it's not necessarily a necessity. The camera looks for honesty and some people don't need to be taught.

When casting a British urban film in 2014, we were looking for the teen versions of our cast who were all London rappers. The teens that we discovered from 'street casting' had this beautiful and believable rawness that the perfectly poised and refined articulation of the drama school graduates could not compete with. Even those actors who had grown up in the same areas, with the same backgrounds as the rappers, had spent years being taught how not to talk 'street' and now we were asking them to undo all of that training. It just didn't work. Perhaps this is a bad example and had both parties been up for posh private school roles then the untrained actors wouldn't have been able to step up to the mark, but perhaps you would expect that in all auditions the drama school graduates would have been ahead of the game. This was not the case.

Being on the other side of the casting table has taught me that it is the essence of a person that wins the role, not the training credentials. Whatever you decide to do, it will be a combination of your talent, appearance, professionalism and, sadly, your profile that will be the key factors in getting you acting roles. Not the training that's written on your CV.

CHAPTER 3

HEADSHOTS AND PHOTOSHOOTS

Photoshoots can be a big part of being an actor so the sooner that you can get comfortable with them the better. Just google any actor you admire, and you will very likely find lots of portrait images of them. Most jobs you get will require some kind of promotional shots, be it movie or theatre posters, press shots or production stills, which aren't always as candid as you'd expect. The most important thing that you need to master is the dreaded headshot. It's not so much the getting your picture taken that makes the whole thing so terrifying, it's that this one picture could be the difference between getting called in for auditions or the CD swiping left. You want this picture to be broad enough to pass you off as every role you are capable of playing. Brutal, isn't it? Not to mention that it can be expensive. A standard headshot photoshoot can set you back between £150-£450 for a one- or two-hour session.

SELECTING A PHOTOGRAPHER

With so many headshot photographers to choose from it can be a little overwhelming but here are some ways to filter down the competition. Start off by looking up your favourite UK based actors and googling who shot their headshots. If you can find these actors' Spotlight profiles, you can usually see the name of the photographer they used underneath the picture. If you have any actor friends and like their pictures you can ask them who they shot with, and if they recommend that photographer. Mandy.com is a really useful tool as you can view lots of different photos taken by the same photographer and see if their work is consistent.

Now you have a shortlist of favourite photographers, decide what your budget is and who works within it. More expensive doesn't necessarily mean better. I once spent £400 on pictures and those images only got me four auditions over a year. They were nice photos, but I hadn't learnt how to work a camera, so they felt really flat and lifeless. I also spent £150 on a lesser-known photographer. I didn't love the images, but that year I was constantly auditioning. Sure, there were probably other factors involved like who was representing me at the time and how my showreel was, but it goes to show that the price doesn't matter. Stick with what you are comfortable with spending and find a package that suits you.

Different photographers use different backgrounds. Some will shoot in a studio whilst others will shoot outdoors, and some will shoot in a mixture of both. You can also look at photos of actors with similar skin tones and hair colours to see what works for them. I think studio photos work better for me, but when it comes to casting photos it's not always about what you like, you have to consider what your agent wants to work with too.

Your agent needs to like your headshot. They are, after all, the people selling you, so they have to like the sales materials that they are using. If you have an agent, ask them if they have any recommendations for photographers. They may even have a good relationship with someone who offers their clients discounted rates. Whenever I sign with a new agent, I will always get a new set of headshots done and go with their recommended photographer. It's my way of proving that I trust their opinion and it helps them become more invested in me too.

PHOTOSHOOT PREPARATION

You've emailed a photographer and agreed on a shoot date and time. Remember, if you're not a morning person then go for an afternoon slot. Try and arrange for a time that works well for you.

Once you have confirmed a date, they might ask for a small non-refundable deposit and will then send you a confirmation email with all of the information that you need to know about your shoot. Please, please read this email two or three times and be absolutely clear on the times, locations and how to get there and if you have any questions then do not be afraid to ask. The last thing you need is a panic before the shoot, when you realise that Hackney Wick Station is not the same as Hackney Central Station and you end up flustered and spending an extra £10 to get a taxi to the right place.

Outfits

For headshots you should only need a selection of tops. Make sure that you plan ahead and always brings extra options. If you have agreed to a three-look package, then bring ten options so that your photographer can tell you what works best on camera. Make it fun and be your own stylist, order a few things online or go to the shops and try on lots of different options. If you don't use them then you can always return them. Usually your photographer will send you an email with what they recommend. No brand logos showing, no outrageous colours or patterns, you should be wearing the clothes, the clothes shouldn't be wearing you.

Women

Anything that shows a bra or bra straps is a no-no. Too much cleavage just doesn't work for headshots. If vests suit you then choose one with thick straps that cover your bra or, better still, bring a variety of jackets, cardigans and long tops. Layering seems to work very well. If you have a certain type of top that suits you, get it in a couple of different colours. Bring different coloured shirts, jumpers and jackets. If you wear glasses, bring them with you too.

Men

Go for a variety of tops, shirts, jumpers and suits and try different colours that suit you. Also try some different necklines: v neck, crew neck, scoop necks or polo shirts. I know a lot of men who have started with a beard and halfway through the shoot they shave it off. You could also change the style of your hair halfway through the shoot.

Jewellery

If you have any piercings, wear them. Keep it simple; studs might be best but bring options if you have them. You might want to do some shots with and without them. A necklace can also look nice but only if you usually wear it. Whatever you do, keep it minimalistic.

Tan and Fake Tan

It's best not to organise a shoot straight after a holiday as you will look quite different when your tan fades. Even the best fake tan can look uneven and streaky on camera.

Hair

If you can change it up halfway through the shoot and find a different look then great. Try some hair up, hair down, a messy bun, for example. Your photographer may also make suggestions about what they think will work for you. Try not to plan a shoot within a few days of going to the hairdressers, unless you can maintain that fresh from the salon look at every casting. Some photographers will have a changing area with straighteners curlers and products for you to use, some wont. It's always better to pack your own just in case and bring a little hairspray even if you don't use it usually. They amount of times photographers have sent me back in the toilets to water down stray hairs is ridiculous. The joke's on them when they find out the smallest inch of moisture turns me into curly sue.

 If the photographer asks you to give your hair a bit of volume, even if it's not how you usually have your hair, go with it, they are usually right. Hair usually looks better on camera when it's big.

Remember: this is your session so make sure you get out of it what you want. Don't be intimidated by the photographer, especially if they've shot famous actors before.

Nails

Actors and models in general should take care of how their hands look. Hands are very important when it comes to advertising products and you may find neutral nails easier to maintain than bright colours which don't look great when chipped. Don't neglect your feet either. You never know when you might be asked to go bare footed during a shoot or rehearsals.

Makeup

Ladies and gents, this won't be the last time I say this but no matter what makeup you wear, as an actor you definitely need foundation and powder that suit your complexion. The camera is merciless and, at the very least, you need a little cover for under-eye bags and any blemishes. Makeup artists are always powdering people off set. Why? Shine just doesn't look good on camera so if you can get in the habit of de-shining yourself you will look better in photos and no one will even be able to notice why. Makeup should be kept simple and natural.

The evening before a shoot, be extra organised and pack a small bag or suitcase. In Appendix 2 you will find a photoshoot check list to help make sure that you don't miss anything out when packing. Plan your route with 30-60 minutes breathing space. You could have a little mock shoot. Try the outfits and hairstyles together and take selfies to show your photographer. It means less time talking and more time shooting on the day. Most importantly, eat healthily, drink lots of water and no alcohol. Do whatever you need to do to wake up feeling relaxed and your best self.

SHOOT DAY

On the day of the shoot make sure you've eaten well and healthily so you are full of energy and feeling great. I usually pack some water and snacks in my bag. Posing for photos surprisingly uses up a lot of energy so you need to look after yourself and stay hydrated.

Headshot photographers may get you in some odd and uncomfortable squatting positions to catch you in the best posture, framing and light during the shoot, so avoid tight clothes and wear something comfortable on your bottoms and feet.

Prep your hair and makeup before you arrive at the shoot and just top it up once you get there. Some photographers run their sessions from home or a studio where there is some kind of dressing room space. Some only shoot outdoors and you might have to get ready in a coffee shop toilet. Either way when you arrive be tidy, respectful and ready to go.

Listen to some uplifting music before the shoot, perhaps something that makes you feel confident. It will really help you to get in the mood and enjoy the shoot. You can even request to play music during the shoot where possible to do so.

When you arrive at the location before the session, be conscious that there could be another shoot in session. If you arrive more than 15 minutes early, grab a coffee in the local café and take some chill time before your session.

Before the shoot the photographer will usually offer you refreshments and you might have a little chat about where you are in your career, who your agent is and the kind of work that you want. Just be as honest as possible here. This will really help them find out what you are looking for from the shoot and enable them to deliver. If you have had headshots previously, they might ask to see them to discuss what you did and didn't like about them and what your best angles are. Now could be a good time to show your mock shoot photos and unpack your wardrobe choices.

Tip: If a photographer is a little negative or blunt about your previous photos, don't be offended. It's all constructive to make sure that your new photographs are an improvement.

THE SHOOT

Now that you're changed and your makeup is looking great, the photographer will put you in position and do a few test shots. This is so they can make sure their camera settings are correct and it will also give you a chance to relax into shooting. Some photographers will show you the pictures as you go, some won't. I personally ask to see the photos to check how my hair and makeup is. I don't want to see all of the photos. The first lot of photos you see might be a little disappointing, don't worry. It takes a while to get going and for the photographer to figure out what works for you. Loosen up, have fun and make love to that camera lens. Weird, but strangely it works.

Cameras are amazing; they really can see your thoughts. If you are uncomfortable or you have something on your mind, they will see it. If there is nothing going on in your mind, the photo will be lifeless. So, work the damn camera. It's all about keeping your mind active. Act out a scene from a movie in your head, express your feelings with your eyes. Run through different emotions like a monologue in your head: happy, enamoured, intrigued, unsure, pleased, proud, confused, joyful, excited, annoyed, betrayed, smouldering, sneaky, smug, sly. Lastly, try passion. Act like you're trying to turn the camera on (I'm telling you it works) and things are progressing until you are getting hot and steamy with the camera. This should bring you into a lovely natural laugh when you realise how ridiculous it is. Remember, these should only be thoughts in your head. Do not pull sexual faces at the photographer, it will definitely creep them out. A model friend also taught me the 'smell the fart technique' where you squint your eyes and take a deep breath in trying to figure out who did it. Not always appropriate in a headshot shoot but fun to throw in there when you've run out of ideas.

A professional photographer will be very patient and give you brilliant direction to get the best out of you. Your job is to let go, trust them and enjoy yourself. Mix it up so you have a variety of moods to choose from. Every time the camera beeps try something slightly different. Be careful not to move during the shot as you will end up with lots of blurry images.

AFTER THE SHOOT

You've done the shoot so where are the photos? Can you post them today? Not so fast. It varies between photographers, but you could be waiting anything from a day or two to two weeks to receive the 'contact sheet.' A contact sheet is a page of small, low resolution thumbnails of the collection of images after the photographer has deleted any dodgy, eyes closed or blurred pictures. From this you should choose your final selection of photos to be edited. You should already know how many images you are getting, depending on your pre-agreed package, but you can always pay extra for additional edits. At this stage the pictures have not been edited or photoshopped so they might not have the glossy wow factor that you were looking for yet, this is all to come once the images have been touched up. Be patient and take your time choosing your final images, it will be worth the wait.

CHOOSING YOUR PHOTOS

Choosing three or so photos out of hundred on a contact sheet can be a very daunting process but it's easy once you know what you are looking for. Don't worry about the stray hairs and spots that have rudely gate crashed your shoot. Your photographer will edit those out later.

1) Go through each of your different looks/outfits and screen shot or write down the numbers that stand out to you. You are looking for photos that look natural, relaxed and where your eyes are engaging.

2) View your shortlist of images together and then start comparing them. Which photos stand out? Who out of these people would you pick to come in for an audition? Remember, your headshot is the first thing a casting director will see before deciding whether or not to ask you to come in for an audition. Make sure your image will stand out next to hundreds of actors. Keep on eliminating until you have your final selection.

3) Send the contact sheet to your agent, actor or filmmaker friends or anyone who might have a good eye for these things. Two or three people should be enough. Ask them which is their favourite and why? From there you can make an educated decision, but usually you should favour your agent's choice. You also want your final photos to be as diverse and different from each other as possible.

4) Time to submit your final selection and relax. Until you have to do it all again next year.

USING YOUR HEADSHOTS

Gone are the days when you would have to print fifty 8x10 inch headshots in black and white before paying for postage and packaging to apply for jobs. Thankfully now everything is digital which is faster and buckets cheaper, however some people still don't make the most out their headshots. These can be your greatest marketing tool. Here is how you can make the most out of your headshots:

1) Upload all of your headshots to all of your casting sites and credit your photographer. Sites might include Spotlight, Mandy. com, Equity, your personal website and IMDB pro. You need to think about managing your brand and stay as consistent as possible across all platforms. Take down any out of date images that look unprofessional or are dated.

2) Email your agents the new images so they have them on record too and can update their own website.

3) Post to social media. Share to your professional accounts on Twitter, LinkedIn, Instagram and your Facebook page. And if you really love them, why not update your profile and cover photos too.

4) Upload to Pinterest. Pinterest basically acts as a Google image search and can be great for broadening your online presence. Create a business account and upload your images. Add your biography in the description page with some hashtags that describe your image and link it to one of your acting profiles.

Tip: Find out from your photographer what your usage rights include. You should have internet and social media usage as a minimum, but if anyone ever wants to do a published article about you, you may need to pay extra or get permission to use the images first.

CREATIVE PHOTOSHOOTS

In this social media age where everything is visual and online, you need to stay ahead of the game and make sure that you are marketing yourself right. Headshot images can be a little ridged for social media and do not always show your personality. We are in the business where seeing is believing so imagine what your future Oscar-winning photoshoot might look like. Classy, stylish, elegant or maybe whacky and bright.

These days it is very easy to create your own photoshoot. You could either hire a professional team including a stylist, photographer and makeup artist or you could do a time for prints shoot (TFP/free shoot) where everyone collaborates on the shoot for practice and you all use the images for your portfolios. Do a little research online or on social media. Don't be afraid to put feelers out there and drop a message to freelancers that you like who are in the early stages of their careers. Whether the shoot works out or not it's always great to make new connections.

If you are the person organising the shoot, then it may be down to you to pay for refreshments or the studio location if you hire one. If you know someone with a cool location, ask if they might let you shoot there for free. If not, you could do a shoot in the park or on the street. Pre-plan exactly what you want so that everyone is on the same page. Use Pinterest and mock up a mood board so that you can communicate with your team and they might send you some ideas too.

This may feel like a lot of information to take on. Though it is great to be prepared don't over think the photoshoot process too much. You only need one great photo and most photographers will keep shooting until you have found something that you are both pleased with and if you're not, you can always book another shoot.

CHAPTER 4

CASTING WEBSITES

Not too long ago, actors were still having to print and mailout their headshots, cover letters and CVs. It was tedious, time consuming and expensive. Now at a few clicks of a button you can throw your hat in the casting ring so there really is no excuse. There is still a small expense to use some of the sites, but it only takes one job to cover a year's worth of membership fees. Some sites do offer a free option, but these are usually only for lower end or unpaid gigs.

Though it might seem unfair having to pay to apply for a job, these companies do provide a very useful and easy to use service, saving you time by connecting proactive actors to potential employers. Even if you don't pay for the subscription, if you have an active profile on the site you may get employers find you in an actor search and contact you directly for a role. Of course, there are no guarantees of landing any jobs here, but you have to be in it to win it and with the right headshot, showreel and at least some credits, your persistence will pay off. It's one of the many necessary outgoings needed for your acting business. It really is a numbers game. The more jobs you apply for, the more likely you are to get cast in a role.

CASTING PROFILES

A complete casting profile will give casting directors and agents all of the information they need to know about you, to help them decide whether they would like to work with you.

1) Headshot: An up-to-date headshot taken by a professional headshot photographer that represents a likeness of you now. Where possible you should arrange a new shoot every one to two years, or every time you do a big change to your image such as your hairstyle or a weight change. The name of the game is for the casting director to recognise you from your photo when you walk through the door. If they don't, then it's time to arrange a headshot update.

2) Credits: The more relevant the credits are for the industry that you are working in, the better, for example theatre credits for theatre jobs, musical theatre credits for musicals and film/tv credits for screen work.

3) Showreel: Showreels are absolutely necessary for anyone wanting to work in film and TV. Once you have gathered a variety of footage that showcases your talent and versatility you can hire someone to cut together your reel. Better still, you can learn to edit the reel yourself. If you only have one or two decent pieces of footage and not enough for a full reel then I would upload those anyway. It's better to have something rather than nothing. Showreels are less relevant for theatre and musical actors. In these cases, casting directors and agents will want to see you in a stage production. Unless professionally filmed, theatre footage is usually not advised.

4) Statistics: Height, eye colour, languages spoken, skills. Whatever you write in this section make sure that you are completely truthful and always keep this information up to date. You could end up wasting a casting director's valuable time and giving yourself and your agent a bad reputation if you are found to have lied to get a job.

Optional
5) Voice Reel: If you want to expand your earning opportunities

this is a great string to add to your bow, especially if you also can speak with a unique accent or language. Always get your voice reels produced at a professional recording studio, even if you own your own recording equipment.

6) Specialist Showreel: If you are also a professional stage combat performer, stunt performer, dancer, comedian or commercials actor and have enough footage for a separate reel, then go for it. Be wary though, you don't want to take away from your acting showreel by following up an intense, award-winning dramatic scene with an insurance commercial.

7) Singing Demos: These are very useful for musical theatre performers. Demos should also be produced at a professional recording studio.

SPOTLIGHT

www.spotlight.com
If nothing else, you must be a member of Spotlight. It is the most important acting industry directory in the UK, used by all the top industry professionals and casting directors. Most agents will only take you on if you are a member. I would estimate that ten per cent of auditions come from my agents' contacts, 15 per cent come from my own contacts and 75 per cent come via the Spotlight platform. Can you really afford to miss out on that? Spotlight offices are based in Leicester Square in London and they also have their own very popular casting studio spaces. There may be a few hoops to jump through before joining, including proving you have had sufficient training and credits, but it's worth it.

There are many other benefits to being a Spotlight member. For example, you reserve your all-important stage name, so no other performer can claim the same name. To double protect your name, make sure that you register it with Equity too. Spotlight also hold free workshops and events and offer showreel editing and audition filming services. My personal favourite is the Spotlight discounts page where you can save money for anything from gym memberships, cinema and theatre tickets to motor services and amusement attractions (these change every so often). Spotlight can be paid for yearly or monthly initially, but only monthly after your first years as a member.

EQUITY

www.equity.org.uk

Equity is the British performers' trade union. It is there to make sure that actors are treated fairly and equally. It protects your rights as a performer and brings all sorts of issues to parliament and other places of influence. If you are an actor, it is definitely worth joining Equity. Not only can you register your stage name so that no one else can use it, if you are ever underpaid you can take it up with the union and they will support you. For example, during the Coronavirus pandemic they gave out grants to out of work members who were struggling with finances. There is also an option to create an online profile and lots of member discounts to take advantage of.

MANDY

www.mandy.com

Mandy is another casting website that I recommend, certainly at the beginning of your career, for building credits. Though I have seen more and more casting directors using it usually for very obscure roles, it is mostly used by independent filmmakers. It can be a great place to meet up and coming filmmakers who are also at the beginnings of their careers and are working with small or no budgets. The downside of this is you may get an amazing lead role in a feature film but due to inexperience and lack of funding, the production never sees the light of day. Still, you gain the credit, hopefully the footage and lots of great connections.

Mandy has a separate division for dancers, entertainers and voiceover artists. If you pay for premium it only covers you for one chosen division. It's also a great tool if you ever decide to produce your own work. You can hire anyone from writers and directors to editors and in some cases they are happy to collaborate to build their credits too.

As a free member you can view the low or unpaid jobs, create your CV and headshot. This is worth doing, especially if you still have very little online presence. If you do opt for premium membership this can be paid weekly or monthly. Mandy has made a great contribution to my career and I have gained so many great connections through the site. You probably won't find any big Hollywood jobs here, but for me work equals work and if you're not getting regular auditions from your agent then Mandy.com can help to fill that gap.

Tip: Look out for membership discounts from other industry sites. I have previously received discount codes for IMDB and Mandy.com from The Actors Guild, WFTV and Shooting People. A month's membership to one of these sites has been known to save you a third off membership fees to another.

Casting websites are a great way to keep the ball rolling but you have to be willing to put the work in. Consistently spending a couple of hours a week submitting for roles will pay off in the end but only if you don't give up .

CHAPTER 5

FIRST CREDITS

If you can get a great agent, lots of professional auditions and paid acting work straight away, congratulations! You are living the dream. But sadly, for most actors that won't be the case. The competition is tough enough between working actors that usually the newcomers, without acting credits or a showreel, won't get a look in. Even if you are fortune enough to get an agent, the auditions could still be few and far between.

When you're starting out as an actor, the more experience you can get the better. I'm not saying you should take any role that you can. If you're not comfortable with playing a meat eating, naked, kitten murderer, then don't take that role. It's true that the more roles you take on and the more experience you get, the pickier you become. Not because you're a diva but because it might be similar to something you have already achieved, and you don't want to miss out on other potential opportunities. Some actors will also pass on certain productions if they are made by students or have a low budget as they don't want to risk being part of something that could turn out to look unprofessional. However, this is a brilliant opportunity to build your credits. It's better to have something on your CV and showreel than nothing at all. Even a year or two without new credits can look a little questionable. Yes, you might end up playing a few dead bodies or policeman/neighbour/friend roles, but if your performance is good then it won't matter if it's not the highest quality production. Your performance will shine through.

And you never know, that young director that you just collaborated with could be the next Spielberg or Tarantino.

PAY RATES

In a dream world we would all get paid fairly for the work we do. Unfortunately, the acting industry is not a dream world. Blockbusters, studios, Westend and network TV jobs might pay you well but there are too many actors and not enough good jobs. It's not a lack of filmmakers, there are thousands who are dying to get their work made, just like there are actors who want acting work. The lack of finance for the arts is the real problem here and the funding that is available is tough to access.

When producers are deciding how much they will be paying their actors, it will depend on their budget. Equity (British actors union) have worked with PACT (Producers Alliance for Cinema and Television) to agree on what rates to pay actors, depending on the production's budget. This information can easily be found online. Low budget films refer to budgets which are less than one million pounds. Shoestring budgets refer to films less than £100k and could be as low as £5k. Aside from music videos, commercials and corporate films which fall under a separate advertising and business category, it is very likely that your first acting job will be under the low to shoestring budget category. The budget may be so small that in order to get the film finished they need to pay the actors a really low fee or even just expenses.

UNPAID/DEFERRED WORK

It can be frustrating being offered below minimum wage or expenses for a long day on set. However, that £30 you get paid to cover your travel and lunch adds up when a filmmaker is paying their whole crew out of their own pocket. Of course, you do not have to love unpaid work or even want to do it, but it doesn't hurt to understand it. To collaborate on a great project for a few days with other like-minded people, which will help drive their career forwards, doesn't hurt. Benefits of collaborations include progressing your career, building credits, practicing your craft, new experiences, building lasting relationships and helping out new filmmakers. It's easy to think the filmmakers are purposely trying to exploit the actors but the truth is there is no pot of gold at the end of the rainbow.

EXTRA WORK

If you are already a Spotlight registered working actor, then extra work is looked down on. Anyone can be an extra. You must not mistake this for being an actor. To be an extra, all you have to do is fill in a form, take a couple of basic photos and you're usually in. Be aware that the acting industry turns its nose up at actors working as extras, even if the jobs are sometimes better paid.

For an out of work actor, being an extra can be torturous. Imagine getting the call. They need you on the set of that big Disney film, starring that really famous actor you love, directed by your most favourite director ever. The night before you get sent a location, a call time and asked your sizes for wardrobe. You get butterflies with excitement; you can barely sleep! The alarm goes off at 4 a.m., it's still dark outside. You make your way to the film studios, it's so glamourous and exciting. They direct you to the green room before you're called in for hair and makeup. As the MUA (makeup artist) tickles you with the powder brush you can't help but think, it just takes one actor to fall ill or get caught up in traffic for them to call out, 'is anyone else an actor in here!' Or you catch the multi-Oscar-winning director's eye, who demands that he's introduced to you this very second because you're perfect for his next movie. This is every extra's dream, but the reality is it just doesn't happen this way.

Instead you will find yourself bundled into a tiny, freezing room with one foldout chair per three people, shouted at and told to shut up. Then you might be made to stand in the rain for three hours before being sent to the back of the catering line. You are told off or reported to the agency if you speak to anyone who is not an extra and renamed according to your physical appearance.

That said, if you have never worked on a big professional TV or movie set before, I encourage you to do at least one day working as an extra. To watch a film crew and actors on set working together, how the different departments interact, the sheer amount of people involved and how every one of them is important, will really blow your mind. You will learn, yes, but most importantly feel what working on a filmset is like.

MODEL AGENCIES

Modelling can often go hand in hand with acting. If you do have a strong look you could consider 'modelling' on the side. There are many varieties of modelling, but I want to focus on high fashion and commercial.

High Fashion

You do have to have that 'model' look. In general, high fashion models will usually be seen on catwalks, music videos, advertising designer brands and in magazines. If you are suitable for high fashion model agencies, you will have to build a portfolio specifically for this type of modelling.

Commercial Modelling

This is essentially 'anyone' looking people. Commercial models are still beautiful and usually have great skin, hair, nails and teeth, but generally it's more about a friendly smile or something quirky, rather than a sexy scowl. Jobs tend to be for everyday high street brands. Though some actors refuse to do advertising, and some people even advise against it as an actor, the money can be great and so can the exposure if you do the right kinds of work.

Model agencies can essentially double up as a 'second agent.' Most model agencies are also non-exclusive, depending on what contract they offer you. The established agencies will have their own personal contacts which your acting agent won't have. Some agents don't want you having more than one acting agent but will be ok with you having a separate model agency as long as no auditions are conflicting. I have worked casting on productions where, for efficiency, we will ask one agency to cast the whole shoot. If being successful is a game of making as many opportunities as possible, it really is worth it to spend a couple of days researching and writing off to all of the relevant agencies. You've got to be in it to win it.

You should NEVER pay to join an agency. If they do ask you to pay to be represented by them, they are most likely NOT legitimate. Agencies will usually take a 10-20 per cent cut of your earnings, this is because they believe they will get you work. If an agency is asking for money upfront, even for admin fees, it is because their clients probably are not making enough money to support the agency and they aren't sure that they will get you any work. Disreputable model agencies in particular are notorious for charging £60-500 for photoshoots or joining fees and then taking a couple of basic images which will not pass as industry standard. I have heard of so many of these instances where people starting out have been ripped off. They have ended up with terrible images and the agencies never get them a single job. I repeat, agencies should work off commission. They should be confident that they can get you work and will take a percentage of your earnings, ONLY once you have been paid for a job. If you have been offered any other deal and want to consider it then do some further research and speak to a model who is already represented by them.

CHAPTER 6

SHOWREELS

When a casting director likes your pictures and is considering you for an audition, the next thing they will do is check to see if you can act. How do they do this? They're going to watch your showreel. If you don't have one, there could be a huge issue. Building a showreel can be a very long process, especially as most producers and directors won't give you a copy of the final work until the project has been released or has finished the 'festival rounds.' Sadly, this could mean it may take months, and in some cases years, to get hold of footage. Luckily these days there some easier alternatives where you can take things into your own hands and have a great showreel within a few months.

SHOWREEL FILMING SERVICES

These have been very popular in the past few years and can be quite efficient if you find the right deal. There are many different packages but essentially most will include a script writing, filming and editing service. First, they will discuss scene ideas and characters with you and then arrange a date to film. Once it is filmed, they will edit the scenes for you. Sounds easy but watch out for the packages and what they entail. Please do your research and ask for feedback from actors who have worked with them first. In most cases, showreel services are just a side hustle for filmmakers so make sure whoever you choose to work with actually has a passion for helping actors, otherwise the work could turn out sloppy and useless.

About ten years ago an acquaintance recommended their brother-in-law who was a director and had just started up a showreel service. I ended up paying nearly £800 for three scenes for which I had to find the locations, props and actors myself. The footage was so basic and carelessly edited that I ended up re-editing the whole thing myself. For the amount of money and work that I put in, I could have produced the scenes or even a short film myself. If you do find a good company to work with then you should end up with results that can pass off as a scene from a real production.

PRODUCE YOUR OWN SCENES

Not the easiest route but certainly the most rewarding and you could end up not only gaining another acting credit, but a writing and producing credit too. Simply come up with a character you would like to play and write a simple duologue scene in an easily accessible location. You could write a monologue but most of the time CDs would prefer to see how you interact on camera with another actor.

Once you have a scene or a few scenes you want to shoot, find your co-star by either reaching out to any actor friends or put a post on Mandy.com. Free additional showreel material should be temptation enough, but you can always offer to pay travel expenses and offer lunch for good measure. For crew you will probably need a self-shooting director and sound recordist, although you could go all out and hire a makeup artist as well. Some crew might work for expenses if they are also looking to build credits or their portfolio. If not, set out whatever budget you feel suitable and either put a post on a film crewing website or get in touch with people who you would like to work with and are within your budget. If you're organised and can shoot the whole thing in a few of hours, you could create something good for £100-£300. You will also need someone to edit the footage and export it in the right format and buy a hard drive big enough to store all of the footage and sound. I recommend that this is all backed up immediately on set and on at least two different hard drives for safety. A self-shooting director might want to edit the work, or you could even learn to edit yourself.

TO SELF-EDIT OR HIRE AN EDITOR?

If you already have great footage but just need it edited, you can either hire someone or learn to do it yourself. Learning to edit has saved me an insane amount of time and money over the years. I'd go as far as to say it's essential to learn how to edit. It's useful not only for creating self-tapes fast but you can also update and create new showreels without spending a penny. These days I can edit a showreel together in 15 minutes. Showreel editing services usually cost between £30-200. To edit myself I use a Mac Book Pro and Final Cut X, not the cheapest of options but well worth it in the long run and very simple to use once you get the hang of it. There are also free editing softwares and apps for phones and tablets. It's really a case of cutting, pasting and chopping in the right places and I have full confidence that with a few online tutorials you will never have to pay anyone to edit your footage again.

GETTING HOLD OF FOOTAGE

You do an acting job and then you get a copy for your showreel. What's so hard about that? You might be surprised at how difficult it can be to get hold of footage. There's the completion of the production itself which could take years, but then if the project is submitted for festivals the footage has to be offline in order to be eligible to take part. Some filmmakers will be very precious about their work which makes it difficult when actors need the footage. This can be understandably frustrating, but we can only do what is in our control.

If a filmmaker is being precious about their work, you could offer to password protect your showreel. Or perhaps they could send you a password protected link to the film footage which you could pass on to anyone who wants to see it. This is a great compromise as they can stay in control and you have something to show. While contacting the director and producer is productive, sometimes even they do not have access to the completed footage and therefore it can be a long and dragged out process. Ask them if they would mind you getting in touch with the editor yourself. If this fails, then revert to creating some new content yourself to fill the gap.

What if the project has already been released but no one has given you a copy? I'm not entirely sure how legal it is but sometimes you have to get down and dirty to get hold of that footage. Sadly, there are a lot of bootleg movie copies that end up online. Not great for the producers, investors and industry as a whole, but great for an ignored actor. Simply go online and download a copy of the movie or tv show. That's it. It might take a while to find a good copy, but it solves that problem at least.

My most recent and favourite of all footage grabbing techniques is the fabulous screen recording tool on my iPhone. I managed to download two commercials in the last month and create my very first commercial reel in minutes. Great for online videos, but not great for anything on a streaming site as you cannot record from them.

Last, but certainly not least, if you have an agent ask them if they can get hold of it for you. You are a team after all and what benefits you, benefits them.

WHAT MAKES A GOOD SHOWREEL?

I have heard many actors ask CDs this question and usually they all give the same answer. Two to three minutes in length is ideal; your showreel should be no longer than that. It should all be about you and your performance. Begin with a scene where you go through a range of emotions and your normal, natural speaking voice is heard. Try and use footage that has good sound and high production value. If you do have a scene with another actor, no matter how famous they are, make sure the focus is you. This is your showreel, not theirs. Montages and music can come across a bit self-indulgent and CDs usually watch them when they want a laugh – their words not mine. Keep it simple with natural with honest performances. I usually start with a simple black card with your name on it and end with your agent's details and your Spotlight pin. If you do this, make sure that when you change agents you update and delete any reels with your old agent's details on them.

The main point of a showreel is to see how you look and sound on camera but most importantly, to see that you can act. It doesn't have to be the most polish showreel, but something is certainly better than nothing.

CHAPTER 7

AGENTS

Agents. That shining beacon, solving all of your acting problems. The hustle is over. Now time to sit back and let someone else do the work for you. Sadly, this is another myth that I would savagely like to bust. Yes, getting an agent is a great achievement and an exciting step in your career but it doesn't make you as a 'product' more desirable. Over the past fifteen years I have been represented by ten different agents, from the unknowns to the super-agents (a super-agent is one of the top ten agents in the UK). Some relationships have been amazing and unfortunately, yes, some have turned sour. It's been a long learning curve but less 'stressful' dealing with or changing agents. When working in casting, we didn't care about who the agent was, and it would never be the difference between bringing in an actor or not. We went by their previous credits, headshot and showreel. If you are right for the part, you are right for the part, so don't let that slow you down if you are unrepresented.

HOW TO GET AN AGENT?

Most agents will only represent you if you are already a member of Spotlight. As discussed earlier, to join Spotlight you need some sort of training or at least a few professional credits and a headshot at the very minimum. In order for an agent to represent you, they will need to see you act, so you will either need to have a showreel or be appearing in a show that they can come and see. In some circumstances they might offer to meet you and ask that you prepare a monologue, although this happens less often now.

If you are in a show or doing a showcase this is the perfect time to get in touch with an agent. It's unlikely that they will travel too far to see a show and most agents are based in London, but it's a great way of starting dialogue with them, especially if you can get hold of any reviews. I did a show at the Barons Court Theatre, an off-Westend small theatre, and invited an agent. He couldn't make the show but called me in for a meeting and ended up signing me anyway. Equally, if you have a film screening, even if it's a short film, if it's at a nice central venue then it's also a great opportunity to invite agents.

When inviting agents to shows ensure they are on the guestlist or their tickets are free and easy to collect. You don't want to worry about tickets, especially if you're on stage that evening or doing a Q&A. If you can't get any complimentary tickets it could be worth buying the agent a ticket or two yourself. Drinks vouchers always go down well too. This same advice can be used when inviting casting directors.

If you have a good showreel on your Spotlight this could be enough to get a follow up meeting for representation. When contacting agents, always address them by their name rather than 'Dear Agent' or 'Dear Sir/Madam.' Make sure the email is as personal as possible. Write a cover letter with a few lines introducing yourself and your greatest acting achievements. Explain that you are contacting them looking for new representation along with any relevant links to work, showreels and your CV.

Tip: Make sure you research the agent that you are applying to. Check their website to see whether they are accepting submissions or if they represent anyone similar to you. There might be a different email for actors seeking representation or special requirements when contacting certain agents.

Keep note of who you have contacted so if you're not successful this time you can try again in a few months. Bear in mind it's a numbers game. Stay open minded and make sure you do your research. Back when I was starting out I would email around fifty agents, now I will streamline it to around ten. It could take a few weeks for them to get back to you. In some cases, if you are unsuccessful, you might not hear from them at all. Don't be discouraged. If none of those are successful, then research a few more agencies and try again. You don't have to make a decision until you meet an agent in person.

MEETING AN AGENT

When meeting an agent for the first time treat it like a business meeting. Get plenty of sleep, make sure you've eaten, leave in good time and arrive around ten minutes early. Pre-plan your outfit, look smart and make an effort. Be comfortable but be you, so consider how you might dress for an audition or job interview. Keep your makeup and hair smart and natural. The first thing they will do is compare you to your headshot to check that you're being marketed the right way. Then there will be a chat where you get to know each other a bit and a Q&A session.

Prepping questions the day before your meeting and figuring out what you want is very useful. The kinds of questions I might ask include the following:

- How did you become an agent?
- Why did you decide to become an agent?
- What kind of roles could you see me doing?
- What kind of jobs would you put me forward for?
- What can I do to improve my Spotlight profile?
- What kind of contacts do you have within the industry?
- How many actors do you represent?
- How many members of staff are at your agency?
- What's the biggest role that you've landed someone?
- How long is your contract?

- Would we do an exclusive or non-exclusive contract?
- What is your commission fee?

Don't be afraid to discuss money and commission, this is a business after all. The tone of this meeting should give you a sense of how your working relationship will be. You do not have to make any decisions on the spot. Make sure that you like and get on with your agent. You will be working very closely together, after all.

Warning: No acting agents should EVER ask for money upfront. This could be a red flag and agents should only work on commission. Do not sign with an acting agent who asks you for any kind of payment upfront including admin fees. Like model agents, they will usually take a 10-20 per cent cut of your earnings.

PROS OF AGENTS

Protection

Actors can be pretty vulnerable, especially at the beginning of their career. A good agent will come with a wealth of experience and be able to suss out what opportunities will be good for you. If you get direct emails about projects, it can be a good idea to direct them to your agent if you are not sure how legitimate the job is. They should also have a good amount of legal knowledge and can make sure that you don't sign yourself into anything dodgy. I once got a lead role in a TV series with a new production company. My agent at the time had a two-week battle with them because they had a section in the contract tying me in to work for them exclusively for a whole year, when I was only being paid for a two month's shoot. I was so excited to have two months of work that I probably would have signed it anyway. My agent wouldn't let me do it. In the end I had to turn the project down. As much as that was hard to do, I did several other great jobs that year and the show I had turned down didn't do too well anyway. Sometimes these things are a blessing in disguise.

Negotiating

When it comes to negotiating money and contract terms, it's best to have someone else to do that for you. It could become a little awkward if you end up having a heated conversation about money with the producer one day and then have to perform a very vulnerable scene in front of them on set the next day. Better to let them get annoyed with your agent for asking for more money, than with you. There have been many occasions that my fees, travel arrangements and per diems have been substantially increased because of my agent's negotiating skills. So, don't worry too much about that 10-20 per cent fee, a good agent will pay for themselves.

Contacts

With a bit of luck your agent will have some good relationships within the business. Especially with casting directors or directors. In this case, the dream would be for them to set up a general meeting for a non-specific role so that they can keep you in mind for future projects. My agent's sister is a casting director, so she sometimes gets a few breakdowns before anyone else. Another agent used to get me invites to premieres and free training memberships. Like any business your network is so vital. If you can tap into your agents' network, then that's a bonus too.

Confidence Boost

Acting can be a lonely career. Non-industry friends can find it difficult to understand and if you haven't got many friends within the industry it can be hard to get the support, so your agent at least will understand your woes. Not that you're going to find a best friend in an agent. One agent turned around to me and started ranting about how actors get confused thinking she's an agony aunt, however it's nice to know that there is someone out there who is on your team and believes in you. There's no denying it, announcing your agent whilst doing your profiles at an audition, or when it comes up in conversation at an awkward networking event, does feel gratifying. After all, you probably jumped through enough hoops to get one.

Chasing Fees

Sometimes payments can get delayed. Delays usually come because productions get their funding in trickles. For example, investors might only give X amount of the budget for pre-production, Y amount of the budget for production and Z for post-production. But if your shoot was on day 1 of 50 and they didn't account for paying you until Z amount had come in, after shoot had wrapped on day 50, then you could unfairly be waiting a long time to get paid. Or you were hired by the production company and they are having delays being paid by their client. This can cause a knock-on effect for your payment. It's no excuse but it can be easier to deal with if you understand why. Luckily, chasing payments is your agent's department. So, if you want to work on the producer's next movie but you haven't been paid for the last one and someone needs to have strong words with the accounts department at least it won't be you. These difficult conversations shouldn't, but could, compromise your on set relationships, so it's best that your agent is left to solve any issues.

There might also be a situation where a big brand who you did a commercial for a couple of years ago wants to run it again and you are due another buyout. Or if you agreed in your contract on a backend cut (percentage) of a movie's profits or are due royalties from a soap re-run. It's your agent's responsibility to make sure that these are followed up. However, it's also a wise move for you to keep a record of these dates too, especially in the case that you decide to change agents.

Finding You Auditions

Finally, she brings up the auditions. Surely this should be top of the list? Well, yes and no. Obviously this is the main thing all actors want from their agent. Expectation-wise it's more sensible and less disappointing if you reprogram your mind to see the auditions as a bonus. You should always be on the lookout for acting opportunities yourself, either by sending out emails, networking, social media or creating your own work. No cruising allowed here, my friends.

Agents should certainly be putting your forward for Spotlight jobs and anything else they find but you should also keep control of your career by working to find auditions too.

CONS OF AGENTS

They Take Money

Yes, your agent will be taking a cut of your work and I'm not going to lie, when you get paid for a 10k job and they take their 20 per cent cut, does it hurt? Yes, of course. But if they got you the job then that's still a whopping 8k that you didn't have in the first place. Without them you might not have been seen for that audition in the first place, so when you think of it like that, that's 8k you wouldn't have got, had it not been for them. Like I said, they do pay for themselves.

Disagreeing on Jobs

Agents can be very persuasive so it's best to check that you're on the same wavelength when it comes to your career. If they want you to build your reputation in TV but then you find yourself a low-paying touring rep company job that will take you away from TV for ten months, there could be issues. Equally, if you get booked for a highly paid commercial but you change your mind because you realise it could clash with the kind of 'brand' you have created for yourself, there could be issues. Like in any working relationship, disagreements are bound to happen. As long as you and your agent have a good working relationship it shouldn't cause too much of an issue. If it does and you feel that a disagreement has affected the way that your agent treats you, perhaps it's time move on.

NEGATIVE AGENT TRAITS

That classic image of an agent depicted in so many movies is of a greedy, intimidating, snooty or dodgy salesperson type who constantly treats their actors badly. Telling them they're washed out or not talented enough or sells their actor a dream and then ignores their calls. I've never personally worked with an agent like this, but I know plenty of people who have.

Careless

If there is some kind of miscommunication then it could end up in a horribly embarrassing situation for you. When I was in my late teens, I was called in for a huge group audition for a BAFTA winning TV series with a famous casting director and my agent had sent me two different audition times. The first email said 2 p.m. start and the second said 2.30 p.m. start so I assumed they had moved me to a different slot, which happens sometimes. Now I would question it, but back then I didn't. So, I turned up to the American Church in Goodge Street at 1.30 p.m. but seeing as I was so early, I went to a café around the corner to have a drink and to ground myself. At 2.10 p.m. I went back thinking I was early, only to be screamed at by the casting director in front of all of the other actors for being late. When I tried to explain the mix up, she snapped back, 'Well change you agent then!' She was right. So, I did. She was also in the wrong for screaming at me like that. If anyone did that to me or to any other actor now, I would report the casting director to Equity or The CDG (Casting Directors Guild). Needless to say, I didn't get the job.

Rude

If for any reason an agent is rude to you, you do not have to accept this behaviour. There is no need for it. Let's face it, we all have bad days and being an agent is a high-pressure job but if someone is continuously rude to you then you should not stand for it. Respect is important in any relationship. If you are not shown it and it is getting you down, don't feel that you have to put up with it.

When I was represented by a 'super-agent' things had gradually been deteriorating. The nail in the coffin for me came when a production manager had gone rogue after having an argument with my producer and sacked (rightfully) from a movie that I was working on. He wanted to be paid for three months of work though he had only done one week, and so to pressure the producer into paying him he started bad mouthing me to my agent. Instead of asking me about the situation, my agent called me shouting, 'This is my agency! I don't want you ruining my reputation that I've taken years to build.' It was ironic that the guy who was hired to protect me had turned on me. After explaining the situation, he laughed it off and said, 'Yes, I thought that it sounded odd.' A few days later, I politely 'said goodbye' to that agent and went back to my old agency who were happy to have me. I also went from three auditions in a year to three a week. These things indeed are a blessing in disguise.

POSITIVE AGENT TRAITS

Communication
The number one thing that makes a good agent is someone who communicates well. They have to relay some pretty important information between yourself and a casting director. Dates, times, locations, contact details, flights. You need someone who is clear and concise at communication. Everyone works differently, so usually it's a case of fitting in with how they run their agency.

Contactable
A good agent will get back to you within 24 hours. As long as you aren't bombarding them weekly with 'where are my auditions?' messages and only contacting them with relevant questions or information. If an agent is going to take leave, they should email ahead with their leave dates so you know in advance, and so you're aware of who you should contact instead.

Friendly
Everyone is different and you will find that some agents are warmer than others but generally your conversations should be polite, friendly and enjoyable.

Honest

If there is a problem, like a double booking, a job gets cancelled or there is an issue with payment, then it is always better that they handle it with transparency, rather than ignoring your messages. Perhaps auditions have slowed down because your last set of headshots aren't quite working for you or your showreel isn't selling you as well as it could. Or maybe it's just quiet for everyone at the moment. You need someone who will be able to talk straight to you about this, and you need to be open and listen.

Time

A phone call every couple of months or a meeting every six months is really not too much to ask for. It's true that in my earlier years as an actor I probably needed a bit more attention as I was building my profile. If you feel you need attention and direction from your agent, they should happily give you it.

Team

It's great to have another person on your team, someone who believes in you and who can take care of the admin, but really you need to be spending that freed up energy in another area of your career whether you're working on your accents, writing or networking.

How your agent behaves is not in your control. How you behave is. Everyone one of these positive and negative traits can be applied to actors too. If you have to, reread both the positive and negative traits lists checking that your behaviour and attitude is in line with this too. Are you reliable? Hardworking? On time? Do you give good notice of holiday and availability? Do you know your lines? Are you professional? If you are all these things, then you know you have done everything that you can to keep this a great relationship which will keep on growing.

CONTRACTS

A long time ago an actor told me, 'Never believe anything until it's in a contract.' This is a great mantra to go by. In such a turbulent industry, where things can change at the drop of a hat, contracts are the reassurance that you need before you go ahead and cancel personal or business plans. If the person who is booking you is not willing to put it in writing, then you may have to question how serious they are. Contracts not only reassure all parties involved, they set out exactly what is required of you so there are no big surprises later down the line.

The contracting stage is also when having a decent agent will come into its own. They will be able to work with you to make sure that you are well treated and fairly compensated for your work. Usually when a contract comes through, your agent will read over it first and then send it over to you once they have given it the all clear. In some cases, they might send you the contract and flag any amendments they suggest and see what you think. When reading a contract yourself, take your time and take notes. If you have any questions or queries discuss these with your agent. If you have a job which includes travelling aboard or staying overnight on location, ensure that everything you require is outlined. I was shooting a low budget feature film in Cyprus for a week. When reading the contract, I flagged up to my agent to see if checked in luggage would be covered as it wasn't specified. It turned out that it wasn't initially, which would have been a drama for me when I arrived to check in. They added it into the contract and I had a smooth check in at the airport. Little things like this don't seem like a big deal but they are worth being clear on from the outset.

Whatever happens, do not sign anything that you do not feel comfortable with. It will only come back to haunt you. It's usually very difficult to renegotiate once the contract is signed. At the same time, do not demand the world. There may be instances where you have to make compromises and if you do agree to compromise, do not flag it up later.

Tip: Watch out for contracts which give someone rights to use images or footage of you 'in perpetuity.' This means forever. I know a beautiful and bright actress who is quickly going from strength to strength in her career. She did a stock footage shoot and earned around £200 for the shoot. She signed the rights over to the photographer in perpetuity and since then those pictures have been sold on to huge companies for international campaigns. Those jobs probably would have earnt her £10k-20k, which she hasn't seen a penny of. I did a campaign along with a very famous Game of Thrones actress. She obviously signed the same in perpetuity contract as me and now our images are still being used in train stations around the country. Not the worst thing ever, but still nice to think that you can keep a little control over your own image.

SUPER-AGENTS

For the first few years of my acting life, whenever I would do a mail out, I would always message the top ten agents or super-agents who represent the world's top actors. Of course, you have to be in it to win it, but it took thirteen years to bag a super-agent and, as mentioned before, the grass isn't always greener on the other side. Are you better off being a big fish in a small pond? Or a small fish in a big pond? Many times I've heard unknown actors say that they struggle to get their super-agents on the phone. I'm not saying it's bad to have a super-agent, I've heard from a super-agent himself the power that they have. If a producer is interested in a famous actor the super-agent might have the power to say yes, you can have this famous actor, if you cast a couple of my unknown actors in smaller roles. This is great news if you have super-agent who is willing to invest time into you. Once you land that super job, they will be magnificent at negotiating your contracts and making sure you are well looked after on and off of set. They can set you up with some great casting director and director meetings, organise invites to premieres and award ceremonies and help you with PR and press.

Yes, if you have that big break or are a rising star then a super-agent is exactly what you need. Mention them at the right audition and the casting director will ask you to pass their love on to them. Actors will be in awe and want to know the secret to how you manged to get one and what it's like. When I was single an actor once confessed that he only went on a date with me after he saw that I was repped by a super-agent, therefore I was probably worth his time (I made a swift exit).

However great having a super-agent is, it seems that the legends are true. Unless you are famous or a continually working actor already, the focus will mostly be on the actors who are making money and every so often you might get thrown a bone. Obviously, everyone's careers are different and if you do get represented by a super-agent, make sure that they treat you well.

SHOULD I LEAVE MY AGENT?

This is such a personal thing and really depends on your history with your agent. If your agent has displayed a lot of the negative traits, then perhaps it could be time for a change. However, if your agent has a lot of the positive agent traits and the problem is a lack of auditions, perhaps it's your photos, showreel or credits that need the upgrade. Rather than placing the blame on external sources, take advantage of the components that you can take control of. Are you being productive enough? Are you putting out the right energy? Is everything up to date? If all of these things are in a good place and you've been with your agent for one or two years already, perhaps it's time to consider other options. Before taking the leap it's definitely worth giving them one last shot. There must have been some good reasons for wanting to be represented by them in the first place so take your time before making that decision, as once you've expressed your interest in leaving, there's no turning back.

Arrange a meeting, in person if possible. At the meeting ask them what they think you can do to improve going forwards. What are their views on the industry right now? What can they do for you in regard to casting director generals or any other meetings? Let this meeting and their actions afterwards help you make your decision. If they request any updates on your side do this as soon as possible and then see how things progress from there. Of course, if you are still unhappy with your agent, or you weren't able to pin your agent down for a meeting, then perhaps it's time to part ways.

LEAVING YOUR AGENT

As an actor, uncomfortable situations come around all too often. Leaving your agent is definitely one of them. I've had to leave agents that I didn't want to because I had more than one and too many conflicts would come up when they both put me up for the same role. Another agent had made one too many mistakes with dates and times and though we had a good run, I knew it was time to move on. I was polite and complimentary, but she still took it personally and asked why I was 'breaking up with her.' I knew this particular agent wouldn't take it well as she'd previously told me that she saw all of her actors as her 'children' and cried for days when they left her. Other agents have agreed that we've had a good run but it's time to move on.

Whatever the reason you decide to leave, you should always treat the agent with as much respect as possible and do it politely and with grace. First of all, check your contract. Do you need to give a month's notice? Are you tied into a year? There is usually a clause which explains the procedure for leaving the agent. In most cases it will be via email. You don't have to be thorough, just a few lines thanking them for all of their hard work so far but unfortunately you feel that it is time to move on and you wish them all the best. Hopefully, they will mutually agree, and you can take them off your Spotlight immediately and self-represent for a while. Like any relationship it's nice to take a little break in between agents and figure out what you really want before rushing and getting involved with another.

I GOT DUMPED BY MY AGENT

In any situation, even if it's a really bad romantic relationship and you're almost at the point of leaving the person anyway, if they get in there first it damn well hurts. It's even worse when you weren't expecting it. If this happens to you, don't worry. It happens to a lot of actors. I believe it's true that when one door shuts another one opens, and it leaves you free for so many exciting new opportunities. Maybe the next agent is the one who's going to get you that breakthrough job whereas your 'ex-agent' wouldn't have got you anything at all. You just have to trust in the process and not take it personally. It is business after all, and we must try to remember this. The agent won't mean to insult you or be cruel (although if they are then report them). They are saying that this business relationship has run its course and it would be better for both of us if we try something new. Be pissed off, be upset, but then pick yourself up and keep going. It might seem like one step back but perhaps it's actually two steps forward.

Having an agent doesn't guarantee that you are going to be working constantly, but having a good agent is a great asset to any actor.

CHAPTER 8

CASTING DIRECTORS

Casting directors: most commonly known as the gate keepers with god-like celebrity status amongst the acting communities. Surprisingly, they are actually humans too and most of them are really lovely people. A lot of CDs actually start out as actors and are pretty compassionate. In fact, when you walk into an audition room, they will want you to be the right person for the role. The sooner they fill the role, the sooner they can get a good night's sleep. CDs come from the business side of the industry. They have to deal with producers and directors wanting 'names.' As much as most CDs would love to find the most talented person for the job, even unknowns, they have to please their clients and make sure that they too are hired again for the next job.

CDs have a tough balancing act between pleasing the people who have hired them and creatively casting the best person for the role. Their job is a very stressful one. Conflicts in schedules, contracts, unfilled roles all have to be managed for a looming filming day. With this in mind, know that it will serve you well to make the casting director's life as easy as possible. Whilst bombarding casting directors with phone calls and emails may not do you any favours, letting them know that you exist in the same way that you would contact an agent might.

I used to feel a lot of anxiety about meeting casting directors and if I ever did a bad job and felt that I had ruined my chance I would panic. I thought that one bad instance could ruin all of my chances in the acting industry. That was until I discovered there are over 250 CDs in the UK alone. The chances of one of them loving you and wanting to bring you in for more work are pretty high. A director friend of mine said, 'your work is not done until you can walk into a room and you don't have to introduce yourself.' Does every casting director in the UK know who you are yet? If not, then you have work to do.

HOW DO YOU GET A CASTING DIRECTOR'S ATTENTION?

Should I send gifts? Or cupcakes with my headshot on? Write a song with their name in it? As much as these are very thoughtful ideas and might get their attention, it probably won't be in a good way. You don't need to do anything gimmicky. A friendly email once every six months to a year, when you have something going on, is more than enough. In most cases they will only want to hear from you when there is a specific role for you or if you apply for a casting. Even for an agent it can take a long time to build a relationship with CDs, but once they know who you are and your work is good, there's no reason why they wouldn't call you in for suitable roles. The best thing that you can do is communicate professionally and respectfully and don't give up. Remember that you are in this for life, so you don't have to rush. They will see you when you are ready for it.

Tip: Don't skip out on the assistant CDs or those who haven't got famous credits. In five years' time they might be casting the next Marvel franchise or HBO series. Start building relationships with those people now, rather than targeting the top CDs all the time. They probably don't receive as many emails so you will have a much better chance at getting your work seen.

Invite Them To A Performance

If you are in a production on stage or have a film screening, send the CD an email and ask if they would like to attend. They may not be able to make it themselves, but they might be able to send an assistant instead. Even if it's just a conversation starter, it will show that you are doing something, and they might remember you next time something suitable comes up. It's a brilliant way of starting a dialogue. Just like with agents attending shows, make sure their tickets are free and easy to access before the show.

Send Links To Your Work

If you have had any work released online this is also a great talking point to introduce yourself. Has something gone up on Netflix? Have you finished your short film that you starred in and produced? Be proud and share any achievements they might be interested in.

Get Organised

Whilst you have to be careful about the legal implications of storing contact details, you could compile a spreadsheet with the names of CDs and keep a record of whether you have seen them already. You could also record what you were seen for, how it went and how the casting director responded to you. In the future when contacting them again you could reference your previous meeting: 'Thank you for shortlisting me for the role in X tv show.'

You will be surprised at how well CDs remember actors. I am always coming across actors who I have previously auditioned. I remember their attitude, their performance and even the questions that they asked. Not everyone, but most of them. There are some actors who I auditioned ten years ago and I still have them in mind for future projects. Actor friends of mine sometimes get offended if I haven't cast them in a role but that's because there have been no roles come up for them. I would love to cast every talented actor in a role, but if the role is not there for them then you simply can't. This is why the more CDs that know who you are, the more chance you have of getting an audition and booking a role.

CASTING DIRECTOR WORKSHOPS

Who better to work on auditions with than CDs themselves? Usually these will consist of a group of actors and you will be assigned a script to perform either in front of the casting director or in front of the group. The session might also involve a Q&A and a chance for you to introduce yourself and tell the casting director what you have done. You will learn lots of great do's and don'ts in these sessions and it's worth attending at least one in your career. Will it get you a role? I have never known anyone to be cast from a CD's workshop but I'm sure it does happen. Be sure to research the casting director before you sign up to the session. It does make you wonder how busy the casting director is if they have time to run these workshops, though some genuinely do just want to help actors. These workshops were banned in America due to people exploiting actors but haven't seemed to cause any issues in the UK. Also remember that these workshops do not guarantee you getting work, but you could learn some skills to improve your audition technique.

If you are active, talented and have good casting profiles then, with consistency and patience, you will start getting noticed by CDs.

CHAPTER 9

AUDITIONS

The late Phillip Seymore Hoffman famously said, 'If you get a chance to act in a room that someone else has paid for, then you're given a free chance to practice your craft.' Although they have a reputation for being a terrifying ordeal, with preparation and organisation, auditions can actually be fun experiences. You get to perform in front of people who want to see you do a great job. That is all there is to it. Well, ok, so the preparation and execution does require some practice and skill. In this chapter, I will give you all of the information that you need to make attending an audition an easy ride.

Getting asked to audition is great. Someone has seen your profile and would love to see if you are the right fit for a role they are casting. Don't take this for granted. No matter what the role is, there are so many actors out there that are dying for this opportunity so make the most of it.

The most important thing to remember is not to be blinded by the lights. Don't get so excited that you imagine this one audition could change the entire course of your life. It's easy to do. Especially when auditioning for lead roles in TV series or international movies. You need to forget about all of that. It's very easy to think that this one job will solve all of your problems. It won't. This is just another job interview so don't get overwhelmed. If you are a person who gets really nervous before auditions, make sure you shift this energy by focusing on the character and scene at hand.

In most cases you will usually only find out about auditions one or two days ahead of time, although there may be occasions where an actor has dropped out and there is a spare slot on the day. This may be difficult when you have other commitments like work, appointments, holidays, personal plans or even sleep. This is why actors need a flexible lifestyle. It might be at such short notice that there isn't time to do any kind of character preparation, if that is your process. As an actor you will sometimes have to make some difficult decisions and sacrifices for your career. If you are at the point where acting opportunities don't come around too often, you may have to prioritise and go that extra mile to avoid missing out when they do arise.

ACCEPTING AN AUDITION

Before accepting an invitation for an audition, whether it is a self-tape or face to face, it is always best to make sure that you want to do this audition. This is not to be mistaken for whether you want the job, as there are many other factors to consider which you might not be told at this stage. As much as it is good to go to as many auditions as possible, if your heart is not in it you could end up doing yourself a disservice and wasting the casting director's time. Before accepting an audition, there are several things to consider:

• Am I available? Production dates given should often be taken with a pinch of salt. I have known filming dates to be pushed back by a full year. However, if you are auditioning for a theatre tour and you are going travelling for three weeks slap bang in the middle of those dates, it's probably not going to work out.

• Have you already been booked on another job? Discuss with your agent whether there could be a potential clash. Your agent should already know about any commitments whether personal or work related. Best to always keep them in the loop to avoid any issues.

- Do you have the right skill set? They're looking a backflipping French judo champion, but you can't tell a French from a German accent and have never even achieved a forward roll in your life. Perhaps skip out of this one and make sure that your agent is aware of your full abilities and that the skills on your CV are not misleading. As much as us actors are talented, if you can't actually do it don't say you can. It can be very embarrassing.

- Is this right for your career? There is no shame in taking student films or no budget work. If you are at the beginning of your career, or even going through a quiet patch, it is a great way of keeping active. After a few notable projects you may only want to work on professional productions. That is completely fine as well. It is your career, after all. There might be nudity involved or the role might be pushing you into a certain type cast. If you don't feel that this is suitable either, then you have every right to make that decision.

- When offered an audition make sure you find out as much information about the production and people involved as possible. Do your research and make sure that it will be worth your time. You might have a bit of a shock if you're used to going up for television roles in Soho but then get an audition in a pub basement in Croydon for a deferred paid student film. I love Croydon, by the way, but you know what I mean. Protect yourself and know exactly what you're getting yourself in for right from the beginning.

- Is the character and script any good? Knowing this is definitely something that comes with time. Learning about writing and storytelling would, of course, help you immensely but there are simpler ways to find this out. Firstly, do you like the character you are auditioning for? It doesn't mean you have to like what they do but do you sympathise with their reasons behind it? Can you relate to them in any way? Do they have a journey, something that they overcome through the story? What is the overall message of the story? Do you believe in it? You could find yourself in a difficult situation when it comes to promoting the project if you have never agreed with its message in the first place. You might be asked similar questions in the audition, so really think about your answers. They might even help you to bag the role.

If the job isn't for you, have a discussion with your agent and see what they have to say as well. If you really can't see yourself doing the job, there is no problem in turning an audition down, although most of the time no doubt it will be an excited, yes.

AUDITION PREPARATIONS

The most important part of an audition is research. It doesn't stop at the character, story and the subject. It is also very important to research the casting director, director, production company, producer, product (for commercials) and attached cast. Watching their previous work could give you a clearer picture of what style they might be looking for. References to their previous work in conversation could earn you brownie points, just be sure that whatever you say is correct and you get your information from a reliable source. It is always useful to know exactly who you are talking to. Knowledge is power, after all.

I would love to tell you the formula for a successful audition but I'm not sure it exists. I have hired acting coaches for auditions and not got jobs. I have been out partying all night (genuinely, I forgot about the recall) and turned up in yesterday's clothes with sick in my hair and still got the role. Definitely NOT what I would ever advise anyone to do, but luckily, I had done my research for the initial audition before going to the bar.

For commercials, corporates and photographic jobs they usually want to just see you, so there's not any character research to do here apart from just the product and any unusual terms or names in the script.

LEARNING LINES

There is no greater benefit to preparation than to learn your lines.

It will give you confidence and freedom to perform. The more you go over them, the more you will learn about what's happening and find new layers to the text. Learning lines is, personally, my worst nightmare. If you have a learning disability and you think that it might affect learning your lines, let your agent know in case the casting director needs to be made aware of this. Find what works best for you and practice, practice, practice.

Tip: I found this brilliant app a few years ago called Line Learner. Gone are the days when I had to ask someone to read with me. It's fast, simple to use and has helped me with so many auditions and jobs. I don't know what I would have done without it. Some CDs will prefer you to have a person reading in with you for an audition but it's a good alternative if no one is available.

WHAT TO WEAR

Come as yourself but a smarter version, unless, of course, the role your auditioning for requires a certain style of dress. Remember, this is essentially a job interview, so you have to make a great impression. Never dress so over the top that it draws attention away from your performance. For commercials bright colours are great. For acting roles, consider similar colours associated with the character. For a period audition I would wear a long skirt and neutral colours. I also recommend that every actor owns a smart, fitted business suit. You can get a good one for around £60 on the high street and it saves any last-minute stress having to borrow items or wearing something that you are not confident in. These days I have two wardrobes: my normal day to day wardrobe and my 'acting wardrobe.'

The most important thing is to feel completely comfortable. If you are doing something that involves movement then wear trainers. I would avoid high heels wherever possible and if you really feel that you need them specifically for a role just have a spare pair in your bag. Either way, make sure that you prepare/clean/iron your outfit the day before the audition so it's one less thing to worry about on the day.

When I was about 20, I was getting very few auditions and never ever booked any of them. So, when a commercial for a well-known bed company came up, I thought that I would take matters into my own hands and dress the part. I got into the audition room and took off my coat. The panel didn't know where to look. The other actor's eyes popped out of his head. I had decided to turn up for the role 'dressed for the part.' Or not. Yes, I turned up to an audition wearing a green satin night dress. Probably in my top three embarrassing audition moments of all time. Not only was I attention seeking and distracting, it completely threw off the other actor and probably messed up his chances too. A director friend of mine used to complain all the time about actors not making an effort when coming to his auditions, as if it made them better artists to dress like they didn't care. People do notice and they appreciate some effort.

Tip: If you are still not sure what to wear, pack an alternative option in your bag. Turn up a little earlier to the audition and get a feel for what other people are wearing. Then change discreetly in the bathroom if necessary. No one wants to see you stripping down to your underwear in the middle of the waiting room.

HAIR AND MAKEUP

Whatever you decide to do, make sure you look like you. CDs don't expect you to be a styling wizard, productions wouldn't spend all of that money on expensive hair and makeup teams if they did. But knowing how to present yourself well is what's important. For me, nothing beats an early night. Eating healthily, lots of water and not drinking alcohol the night before. A bit of powder to get rid of any shine and hairspray for any stray hairs. Fifteen years ago, I was putting big black circles around my eyes and poker straightening my hair, these days I go for simple and natural makeup and neatly tie my hair out of my face. The latter is definitely what books me jobs.

Tip: Mac makeup has a membership scheme which offers a 25 per cent discount off products for performers. Visit the Mac website to register.

WHAT TO BRING TO THE AUDITION

Here is a list of the main things that I recommend that you should bring to an audition. You also will find a more detailed check list in Appendix 3.

- Pack a copy of the script, stapled and highlighted so that it's in the right order.
- A bottle of water and a snack of some kind for energy levels and so that your stomach doesn't rumble.
- A portable charger in case your phone runs out of battery and you need Google Maps to get there.
- Headphones to listen to music, block out the world or listen to your lines.
- Deodorant, hairspray, makeup bag and powder.
- Any costume pieces that you may have been asked to provide.

Tip: Make sure you have the full address and post code, know what you are auditioning for and the name of the person you are seeing. Turning up to an audition with any of this information missing could put you in a sticky situation if the receptionist is running five different auditions at once, yet so many people do it. Next time you are at an audition watch how many people don't have this information and make sure you are not one of them.

VOCAL WARM UPS

Warming up your voice before an audition and also going on set will prevent word stumbles and help you to speak clearly. It is also very important to protect and strengthen the vocal muscles so that you don't lose your voice. There are many diction exercises online. Warming up 20-30 minutes before and audition is ideal. I will usually pretend to be speaking on the phone, reciting tongue twisters to myself or running over lines.

ARRIVING AT THE AUDITION

If you want to guarantee being somewhere on time, allow an extra hour. 30 minutes is not always enough time, especially in London. You never know what can happen; forgetting your keys, leaving your phone somewhere, your phone breaking, disturbances on transport, turning up to the wrong address, going to the wrong tube station, bomb scares or roadworks. Not that you will, hopefully, ever experience more than one of these dramas in a day. These are just some of the things that you could experience, and that I have experienced on the way to an audition.

I remember a time when I was running thirty minutes early for an audition, sitting on the Piccadilly line with one stop to go, and I got held at a red light for thirty minutes making me late. I turned up at the right address only to find out that my agent had given me the wrong address, thirty minutes before an audition. I rang my agent and was told she had given me the wrong address and I had to run across town. Out of breath and sweaty vibes are not a good look (or smell). Although sitting in a waiting room for an hour isn't ideal either. Instead, when you arrive, check in with the receptionist to be sure you are in the right place. Then let them know that you will come back ten minutes before your audition time and go and wait in a nearby coffee shop or park to ground yourself. If you are going to an audition venue that you go to regularly then aim to arrive fifteen minutes early.

Tip: Have all of your agent's contact details and all of your sizes stored in one place on your phone. It will make filling in application forms before the audition a much quicker process. Store a picture of your passport in your phone, just in case this is ever requested for international jobs.

GROUNDING BEFORE AN AUDITION

After checking in with the receptionist, try and find a seat as far away from other actors as possible. Take your coat and bag off, turn off your phone and go to the bathroom for any last-minute hair and makeup checks. Then take your seat and begin grounding.

Grounding is such an important process before an audition. This is where you let go of the stress of the journey and anything going on in your life. Have a pep talk in your head about how amazing you are. You are an individual. There is no one else like you or who can do what you can do. No matter what happens in that audition room you have done everything in your power to give the best performance that you can. There are so many things that are out of your control but doing your best is not one of them. Make yourself proud and leave a great impression so that they want to invite you back for future auditions.

Grounding doesn't have to be done in the waiting room. You can do it walking down the street or sitting in a park or café. Wear your headphones. You don't have to play any music, but it will shut you off from the world for a bit. If you need to get into a certain mood music can help. I find movie soundtracks are great to listen to right before an audition, or anything that your character might listen to, to put yourself inside their mind. If you are still shaky on your lines you can run them through on the line learner app. When I get to the waiting room, I will usually give in to the fact that I either know the lines or I don't and there's not much more I can do. If you do need a little uplift in energy, play some music although very quietly so as not to disturb the other actors or miss your name being called out. Some actors love to chat in the waiting room, especially if they run into someone that they know. If this is you, then be considerate of other actors, it's usually better to keep conversations to a minimum and maybe arrange to chat outside after. Commercial castings are often a bit more relaxed as there's usually no lines to memorise but either way, think of others. Don't let the adrenaline take over and focus.

Tip: Physical and vocal warmups should either be done at

home, on the journey or outside of the building as much as possible. You could do tongue twisters to avoid stumbles, or quietly go over your lines. For accents you can mumble the lines quietly under your breath before going into the room, as long as you are not disturbing others.

WHAT IF I'M LATE?

Sometimes these things are out of our control and as long as we know that we did everything to make sure this doesn't happen regularly, we can't do any more than that. In the rare occasion that you are late, call your agent and ask them to apologise and pass the message on that you are running a bit behind. If you booked the audition directly then message or email your contact and advise them when you might arrive.

In a normal situation, if you were meeting your friends or family for dinner, it would be rude not to apologise for running late. In an audition situation if a panel are seeing thirty to one hundred people in one day, they might not notice. If they don't, do not be the one to tell them. Walking in the door flustered and going on about how it wasn't your fault and you're not usually late is going to bring a weird energy into the room. Firstly, for yourself, because you're asking for forgiveness and giving yourself a low status. When you walk into the room, you and the panel are equals, keep it this way. Secondly, this will probably make them feel uncomfortable, especially if they hadn't noticed in the first place. Unless it's a one on one meeting or they raise the subject of lateness, just act like it never happened and focus on your performance. Good actors are also discreet actors.

WALKING INTO AN AUDITION ROOM

Walking into a room should seem like a simple enough task but sometimes it can be the most daunting part of the whole audition. You are walking into a room full of people who are there to judge you. There are cameras and lighting and it's all very intimidating. In this moment you are not the character. You are you. Walking into a room and wanting to win everyone over. It could be very tempting to walk in the room and shake everyone's hands and to ask their names. To crack a joke or say something because laughter is good, right? Laughter means they like you. Well, laughter can also be awkward and uncomfortable if it's forced. As much as some people are naturally very charismatic and can get away with it, for most people, myself included, it can come across as a little too try-hard and may make the casting team nervous that you could be a little loud and annoying on set.

When walking into an audition room the best thing to do is just that. Smile and say hello with eye contact and walk to the centre of the room, usually facing the panel, and let them take the lead. There will usually be a marker on the floor so that you know exactly where to stand. There might also be a chair nearby, if you need it. Wait until after any introduction before asking if they mind if you use it or not.

Tip: Where safe to do so, leave your coat and belongings in the waiting area or just by the door. There's nothing worse than faffing around as you come in to the audition room and asking where to put them. It's just not a great use of time when you have such a small amount in the room. Since doing this, it has made my whole audition experience so much smoother. You don't want to be the person who smashes their audition and then has to sneakily tiptoe back in the room to get their umbrella. If it's a long and complicated scene you might also want to bring the script in with you in case you need a prompt but try your best never to look at it. If there's a lot of screaming and shouting involved or it's a longer recall session, you might also bring a bottle of water in with you. Just try not to forget it on the way out.

SLATE

An actor's 'slate' is simply introducing yourself to the camera and putting any information that the casting director might need on record. Typically, you will be asked to stand on a marker in front of the camera. You will hear a voice call across the room, 'When you're ready, say your name and agent to camera and give us your profiles.' Pretty baffling for a novice, a little awkward for a beginner but water off of a duck's back for an expert. To 'slate' is a very simple process but takes a little practice. Saying your name and agent to camera should be pretty straight forwards. If you go by a stage name, make sure that is the name you always say. If you don't have an agent either say 'self-represented' or if they found you through Spotlight then say 'in the care of Spotlight.' 'Profiles' means they also want to see your side profiles, which is what you look like from the side. To do this, face the camera and then simply and smoothly turn 45 degrees to the right, pause a moment and then turn back 90 degrees, the way you came, via the camera. Pause a moment again and then turn back 45 degrees to the centre and smile.

The casting director may also want to see your hands. In both circumstances, raise both of your hands to shoulder height to show them to the camera. Show both sides and return your hands back to resting position. If you have long hair, you might be asked to hold or push it away from your shoulders during profiles so that they can have a good look at your posture and body shape. Don't worry, this is not necessarily a posture test, more a chance to see what you look like from all sides.

During the slate you might be asked additional questions such as:
- How tall are you?
- Where are you based?
- What is your ethnic origin?
- Have you done any conflicting jobs?
- Are you available for the shoot dates?
- Do you have any pets?
- Do you have a driving licence?

Every CD has their own process and each casting will be a unique experience. It is also proof that you can listen and answer simple questions directly without causing a fuss. Although you are not acting, this is still part of the interview so treat it like one and make a good impression.

THE AUDITION

You've put the work in, now it's time to give it everything you've got. Be focused, be in the moment, be vulnerable. Enjoy yourself and remember, no matter what happens, do not apologise. This means both apologising verbally but also physically. Us actors are extremely self-critical creatures and we thrive off applause and congratulations. When we don't get it, and in auditions we are very unlikely to, even if you gave the best audition of the day, we might feel like we have done something wrong. Your body language and attitude could change, which in turn might take from what you have just done. Don't let this happen. Remember what I said about the jumping over the rope exercise? It is the same principle. What you do in the audition is what you have done. Be proud of that, regardless of any expressions or comments from the panel. Try not to read in to any comments you might get.

If you forget a line or stumble, which we all do at some point, try to carry on. On a film or tv set it is the director's job to stop the scene, never the actors. You will need to keep going until you hear 'cut!' The camera is a magical thing. It may seem that the whole scene has been messed up, but what you are now doing could be beautiful, so keep it going. If it's not, the panel will let you know.

If you struggle on the first couple of lines, then it is usually possible to ask to start again and the panel will be understanding. Try not to take too long about it. Some people are more understanding than others and it's usually best to leave it for them to ask you to try again, unless you really cannot get through the scene. NEVER ask to do it all again. From sitting on an audition panel, I can confidently say that asking to 'have another go' is a no no. There are a million ways that you could do an audition, but the simple fact is, unless they have asked you to do it again, they don't need to see it again.

When casting a feature film a few years ago, I found if someone walked into an audition and they were amazing, we probably wouldn't need to see them do it again. This didn't mean they had the role, because the next person might be equally brilliant but more suited to the role. We also saw auditions we loved, and the actors had what we were looking for, but they didn't quite interpret the script in the way we wanted to see it. In that case, we might have asked them to do it again. Once, twice, even three times. Does it mean they got the role? No. Yet another person might come in the door and smash it out the park. Perhaps the panel could not contain themselves and let out a 'That was great! Can we please see that again?' because the performance was so good that we needed to see it again. Did that actor get the part? No.

So, who did get the part? Well, the actor with a massive online following who had originally been offered the role but had said no and then changed their mind a week later. None of the actors who auditioned knew this. They were probably left thinking, 'that film audition went well [or didn't go well] because they asked me to do it three times...' The truth was, 95 per cent of the actors that we saw were extremely talented and could have done the job really well. But we couldn't have 25 actors to do one role. We had to pick one. In this case, the producer's need for someone who could bring in an audience won the role. If that hadn't happened and we had to choose from another actor that had auditioned, there would have been nothing that the actors could have done to convince us to cast them. Each actor is so different, even those with the same cast types.

Say you have two actors going for the same thug role. They might be similar in stature, ethnicity and almost identical but their natures and souls are completely different. Even if they were both fantastic actors, one would have been more that part, just because they naturally had something about them that fitted. Something that you can't tell from a headshot or even a showreel. It's like dating apps; you can never really tell if someone is right for you until you meet them in person. It's the essence of an actor which can really win them the role. The truth is it really is luck. That you are in the right place, at the right time and the person that they are looking for is you.

I hope that this gives you comfort and relieves the pressure. The best thing that you can bring to an audition is vulnerability. So, take the pressure off from trying to control the casting panels' decisions and just give a great performance. I'm not saying you shouldn't try, because what if this role IS right for you and you come in with a bad attitude and rude behaviour. Will they still hire you? Probably not if they have 24 other great options. The best way to look at it is to remember there's nothing you can do to persuade them, but there's lots of things that you can do to put them off. So, if you can't control whether someone wants you for a part or not, what can you do? Make sure that you are up for as many roles as possible, and that every person who is casting knows who you are.

DONT SPEAK UNLESS SPOKEN TO

This really is erring on the side of caution. If you have a bubbly happy personality, then of course be yourself. You just want to avoid talking yourself out of a role. Especially if you're in a first round and it's a very busy casting. Being too chatty could be irritating, you don't want to risk getting cut for that reason. Recalls can be more relaxed and might involve a little more conversation. Keep all communication friendly, pleasant, concise and on topic.

CASTING PANELS GET NERVOUS TOO

Bizarrely enough this is true. There can be a lot of pressure to lead the room and not everyone in the casting room is a seasoned veteran. Sometimes casting assistants are running the casting or the client could be in the room, who has never attended a casting before (they are usually recognisable because they're eating a sandwich, playing on their phone or undermining the casting director). The casting team could be dealing with other pressures from the casting office or technical issues. To change the energy and relieve your own nerves, before going into an audition room try to put the casting directors at ease. Walk in with a big and friendly smile and give them time to pull themselves together.

AFTER THE AUDITION

Let it go, let it goooooo! No, seriously. Just let it go. CDs don't have the time to give everyone feedback and even if they did it probably wouldn't be that helpful anyway. What if it was because or your height, ethnicity, age or they just didn't see you in that role? Surely you don't need to know something thing that might give you a complex just because this one role wasn't the right one for you. You're most likely going to get more no's than yes's in the early stages of your career. That could be a whole load of negative feedback that you simply do not need to know. Be proud of yourself and congratulate yourself on having done your very best. You obviously have a great casting profile and out of thousands of actors you were asked to perform for the panel. Treat yourself. Praise yourself. The rest is out of your hands. What is in your hands is staying busy and lining up the next audition.

GROUP AUDITIONS

You are most likely to come across group auditions when auditioning for theatre productions or drama schools. In some cases, you might be given a name badge and number. Yes, it's a bit like being in a herd of cattle, but when seeing so many people the casting team have to stay organised and identify everyone. In these situations, they are most likely looking to see how you interact with other actors. In some cases, you might be asked to perform scenes or monologues in front of everyone in the room including auditionees. Although it sounds terrifying, you have to remember that everyone is in the same boat and usually very supportive. You get to watch other talented actors, make some acquaintances and pick up some performance ideas from the other auditionees.

AUDITIONING WITH OTHER ACTORS

Believe it or not, it's not actually a competition. How can it be when everyone is an individual? On occasion you might be asked to do an audition with another actor. Don't try to be the loudest, the funniest or the one who talks the most. Be courteous, respectful, supportive and wait your turn. If you are in the room together, just the two of you, the odds are you are probably going for different characters or there is more than one role being cast. Don't worry if they are showing off a little, if you are noticing it, the CDs will as well. They will have seen it a million times before and you will probably get brownie points for gracefully going along with it. It's not ideal, but don't leave the room annoyed because someone stole your thunder. Stay calm and remember that as well as auditioning for this role, you want the CD to call you in again. Don't sabotage your chances by reacting in a negative way. This situation is, of course, very rare. In most cases you will end up in the room with another brilliantly talented actor. You will bounce off each other, be in the moment and find things from the text that you didn't see before. If nothing else, you will leave the room with an extremely positive experience. Working and vibing with other people is one of the most fun parts of being an actor.

RECALLS

Recalls are certainly something to be proud of. It means they like you and what you did, and they want to see you again. Although excellent news, it's not time to sing it from the roof tops just yet. You don't know how many other people have been shortlisted. It could be anything from two people to twenty actors. For bigger jobs it could be more. It might sound strange but try to style and dress yourself the same way you did at the first audition. If it ain't broke, don't fix it. Whatever you did the first time worked. If there's something they didn't like or want to change, mostly likely they will let you know prior to the audition. At this stage they might also introduce a new scene or a skill that they would like to see from you. If it's a skill, then you would have been warned of this requirement prior to the first audition. Revisit the original scene and make sure you still remember those lines without being too over rehearsed, just in case they decide to spring it on you as well. At this stage you're in a really good place so I would also do a bit more character preparation and extensive research where you can. Now is the time to cancel dinner plans or prior appointments and definitely get a good night's sleep.

PENCILLED

Amazing! You got pencilled! The casting team think you would be perfect for the job and they want to work with you...but also, there is someone else who would be amazing for the job and they want to work with them too. Or maybe a few people... The good news is that usually at this stage your job is done, audition-wise anyway. They have seen all that they need to see and now just have to make the decision and get the terms agreed and the contract signed. Or perhaps the date has changed or there's been a delay in production, so they're keeping you on hold but don't want to send contracts out just yet. It's like they're on holiday and you're a sunbed and they've thrown a towel on you so no one else can sit on you, but they are not committing to sitting on you either. The main thing is that they want to sit on you...I mean work with you.

Now, this is not always the case but when I am pencilled for my own sanity, I just assume that I am the side chick. The CD likes me, but maybe they like someone else a little bit more and are going through the negotiations and contracts with them first. There are lots of things that can go wrong when booking an actor. For example, they could have lied on their casting form, saying they were available on that date and they weren't, or that they had a clean driver's licence and they didn't, or they could have an expired passport. This is why it is very important not to lie on a casting form. Not so good for the CD, the agent or the actor in question, but brilliant news if you are on a pencil.

No two auditions are ever the same, just as no two actors are ever the same so enjoy each unique experience. You can't control whether you book this job but as long as you are well prepared then you will still be in with a chance of booking the next one.

CHAPTER 10

SELF-TAPES

As humanity drowns even deeper in the rabbit hole of technology, so follows the acting industry. I'm talking about the rise of the self-tape, a process where actors record the auditions themselves and virtually send it to the casting director. It's not a bad thing. There are many advantages when it comes to efficiency and saving time and money. If anything, I take a sigh of relief when I don't have to rearrange commitments, trudge through London's rush hour and deal with the pressure of getting the audition right in one go. With self-taping you can have as many go's as you like. You are in control of what the casting director sees because you are producing your own audition. Of course, meeting a CD in person is much more valuable and if you ever have the choice then you should always choose a face to face audition instead. You show much more commitment by showing up in person, and human connection is still something that technology has not managed to replicate...yet. Some people love technology, some people don't. If you are the latter that is absolutely fine, but if you can't beat them then you might as well join them.

PROS OF SELF-TAPING

- You can do it from home, saving time and money travelling to an audition.
- You get to take have as many takes as you like and do it in your own time. You can keep on going until you are happy.
- You can audition for national and international projects,

opening up new opportunities.
- The casting director is able to see more people than they would if they were holding a live audition.
- No allocated time slots. Just a deadline to send the tape by, so no need to cancel or rearrange other work or appointments.

CONS OF SELF-TAPING
- You don't get to meet the casting director, it's all one sided so you miss out on building a real connection with them.
- Technology can be temperamental and technical issues can be time consuming.
- Potentially more actors able to audition.
- No external direction.
- It can be difficult and distracting if you don't have a suitable filming space for noise and backdrop.

SIMPLE SETUP
For the most simplistic audition tape set up you will need:
- Either a phone, tablet or laptop with videotaping capabilities.
- Device stand.
- Editing app.
- Natural light or good lighting.
- A plain background, preferably light.
- Someone to read with you or an app like line learner.

According to casting directors, you don't need a full studio set up. The most important thing is a clear head and shoulder shot, where you are well lit, and your voice is heard clearly without any background sound. As self-taping is becoming more and more popular, many actors have upgraded to a full professional setup. When the bar is being set so high, you wouldn't want a bad quality tape to disqualify you from a job. If you are in this for the long term then it is worth investing in a more professional set up.

ADVANCED SETUP
For a more advanced and professionally shot audition tape, I would

suggest the following equipment:
- A DSLR camera.
- Camera stand which can extend to your standing height.
- Professional lights (I personally use two light boxes to ensure lighting is even and minimise shadows).
- A memory card.
- A laptop and editing program.
- A plain background or photography backdrop.
- Someone to read with you or an app like line learner.

Don't feel that you have to buy the most expensive products. Do your research and find out what is best for you as well as shopping around for a good deal.

Tip: Always make sure that you have a charged camera battery and there is space on your memory card. It can be quite frustrating if the camera cuts out midway through a take. If possible, have a spare of each, ready as a backup.

SETTING UP FOR A SELF-TAPE

First of all, you're going to need a quiet space where you are not going to be disturbed for at least an hour. Somewhere with a plain, light/white/pastel background would be ideal. If you don't have this, you could look into purchasing a photography backdrop, just make sure that you have somewhere to store it and it does not look cheap quality on camera or covered in creases.

Lights, camera, action. There is a reason why lights come first. Lighting is so important and good lighting will make a huge difference to how you look on screen. Two light boxes either side of the camera will light up your face beautifully, but nothing beats sunlight. If you can find a nicely lit spot facing the sun so that there are no shadows on your face, then you are on to a winner. However, if the lighting is too bright it will drown your features out. To avoid this, move your light boxes back a little or avoid shooting at sunrise or sunset when the sun is at its harshest.

Decide whether you are going to be sitting down or standing up during the scenes. Frame yourself by positioning the camera/device and adjusting the height and angle of the stand. For more intimate and static scenes, you want to frame your head and shoulders with a bit of space above your head, so that your face takes the focus on screen. For scenes where there is a lot more action or movement involved you might want to go for a wider shot and try shooting from the waist up. There are two ways of making your frame wider (bigger) or tighter (smaller). To go wider you can either zoom out or move the camera backwards. To go tighter, either zoom in our move the camera closer. Either way you want to keep the camera at head height, so the casting team doesn't have to stare up your nostrils or look down on you. You might even need a full body shot which will require a lot more space. This will usually be requested specifically from the CD, but in most cases you will just need a simple shoulders and head shot.

You also need to make sure that the camera is in focus. Most phones and devices will have will have autofocus, so you won't have to worry about this too much. When shooting self-tapes alone you can set the camera on selfie mode to check that you are in frame. If you do this, I recommend that you cover the screen once you are ready to shoot so you can concentrate on your performance rather than keeping an eye on what you look like. Some cameras need to be manually focused, meaning unless you adjust the focus you could end up all blurry. To do this, if possible, flip the camera display screen so that you can view it from sitting in front of the camera. Put your hand roughly where your face will be, adjust the focus until your hand is as sharp in focus as it can be and then press record and step into place to start the scene. Self-tapes are great practice for learning what works and what doesn't on camera. Once you get on a real film set the Director of Photography (DOP) and director will love you for asking where edge of frame is and being aware of how to stay in frame, which will save everyone shooting valuable time.

Check out Appendix 4 where I have complied a detailed check list which takes you from the start to finish of recording a self tape.

IDENTS

Though not always essential, when requested you will need to begin your tape with an ident. This should be filmed in a mid-shot (from the waist upwards) and looking down the camera lens. 'Hello, my name is...I am represented by...and I am reading for the role of...' If you are doing a tape with an accent, then do the ident in that same accent. Then, give your side profiles like you would in an in-person audition.

In some cases, the CD might request that you also include a full-length shot. If you are recording alone, you can take this by pressing record, stepping into shot and holding for a few moments and stopping the recording. You can edit this into your final audition tape after you have shot your audition scenes. If it's a commercial, they may ask to see your hands as well. Any other specific requirements will be requested when you are sent the script. Make sure that you follow any instructions given for your self-tapes as best you can.

Tip: Stay in character for an extra five to ten seconds once the scene has finished. It might feel a bit strange, but you will thank yourself for it when it comes to editing your tape together. You will end up with a nice moment, rather than an abruptly cut short scene because you jumped up to stop the recording.

SELF DIRECTING

In between takes, playback the scene you have just shot. Is your acting too theatrical? Do you need to tone it down? Have you tried it several different ways? Some people don't like watching themselves back, but how can you improve if you don't see what you are doing? Don't get too distracted about what you look like. It's very tempting to choose the shot where your hair looks the nicest, but that's not what a CD or director is looking for. Look for an honest, natural performance and mix things up until you find it. If you noticeably trip on a line or fall out of character, then shoot the scene again. It might be a pain at the time, but you will thank yourself for it later. Strive to get a take of a performance that looks as though it could be a scene from the movie/show itself.

SHOULD YOU SEND SEVERAL DIFFERENT TAKES OF THE SAME SCENE?

I have heard casting directors respond to this question many times and the general consensus is, it depends. If you can do two takes that are very different then yes. If they are very similar, then there is not much point.

EDITING SELF-TAPES

When editing a self-tape, you should start with the ident. Then cut straight in to your first and second scenes. Don't worry about fancy transitions between takes. Just cut the scenes together and trim the beginning and end of the scenes of any moments where you are out of character. Each entire scene should be recorded in one take. Do not cut between different takes in a single scene.

LABELLING SELF-TAPES

This is extremely important. At the very minimum it should include your NAME, AGENT and PRODUCTION/ROLE that you are going for. I have heard of casting directors deleting self-tapes without even watching them because they weren't properly labelled. During the Coronavirus lockdown in 2020, a self-tape casting went up and everyone I knew went up for it because the fee was so high and the breakdown was so vague. So many people applied that it was impossible for the CD to watch them all, so they narrowed it down by deleting those that had not been labelled properly. No one wants to spend two hours on an audition tape for it not to be watched. Do yourself a favour and read exactly how they want you to label it. Even worse, they could see your self-tape and love you but if it's not labelled properly they may not be able to contact you. The combination of the ident and the correct labels will guarantee that the CD will know exactly who you are and how to contact you.

EXPORTING SELF-TAPES

Once you have edited and labelled your self-tape, you need to export it. The most popular way to do this is as either a MOV or an MP4 file. You also want to export it at the highest quality, but not so high that it's going to take forever to upload. I find that 540p, 720p and 1020p are all acceptable for self-tapes but if you can do 1020p without crashing your computer then go for that.

UPLOADING SELF-TAPES

There are several ways of uploading self-tapes so check how the casting director has requested to see it. CDs' inboxes are busy enough at the best of times, therefore they probably won't want to receive your full audition tape via email. The best ways to send tapes are the following:

• Upload the video to YouTube or Vimeo and send the link to your agent to forward or send it directly to the casting director. Make sure you set the video to 'private' or 'hidden' and make it password protected. All audition scripts should be kept private. Never post an audition tape for the public or to social media. The script could be top secret and if you share it, it could end up being a damaging situation for yourself, your agent, the casting director and the production.

• Send via WeTransfer. My personal favourite as it is a fast and easy process without issues of giving the wrong passwords etc. A basic account is free to send files up to a certain size. Once uploaded you can pass on the link to your agent or direct to the CD. WeTransfer will also send you a notification once the recipient has opened the file.

• Upload your tape to a casting site if requested by the CD. You will usually be given a job reference and have to create an online profile.

CHAPTER 11

CHARACTER PREPARATION

'An actor's job is to know their lines and show up on time.' Let this quote remind you that this is the very least you need to do when turning up to an acting job. Every actor has their own approach to preparing for roles. In your early years as an actor, it is important to try out different techniques and see what works for you.

During your drama training you will usually explore a variety of methods, although some schools have a set methodology that they teach. I would like to share with you how I like to prepare for roles. Of all of the techniques I do prefer method acting, but not to the extent where I'm compromising my personal life or making others feel uncomfortable. I keep my mind in a safe place, whilst building a strong emotional connection to the character. To learn about the character, I will dissect the script and answer a series of questions. As a bonus, I have shared all of my character questions in Appendix 1. Next time you are working on a character, why not try them out yourself?

CHARACTER RESEARCH AND WORKING WITH THE SCRIPT

When booking a role, it is very important to have a meeting or, at the very least, a phone call with the director to ensure that you are both on the same wavelength when it comes to the direction of the character. Here, the director might tell you some information about the character that you didn't know before, and help you fill in the bigger picture about what their contribution to the story is. If you are working from a script which was originally a book, I would encourage you to read that too. There may be useful information about your character, which may have been cut from the script version.

Read through the script a couple of times and highlight both your lines and your actions. It might sound strange to highlight your actions, but vital pieces of information could come from a single look or movement. In a good script, every moment will contribute to moving the story forwards. You shouldn't take anything for granted. There is not always time for rehearsals, so you have to be as prepared and thorough as possible. Use everything that the script has given you.

Note what other characters say about you. There is a difference between who your character thinks they are and who other characters think your character is. You need to join up the dots when creating your character. Not everything that is said about your character by themselves or others is true either, but it will help you to understand your status and relationships by knowing all of this information.

You may come across words or terms that you have never heard of before. Write these down and research them. When it comes to the day of your performance, you need to make sure that the words on that page flow out of your mouth as if they are your own. If you find that you can't seem to make a certain phrase or word work, do not be afraid to get in touch with the director who will be more than happy to solve the problem with you.

Once I have squeezed as much information as possible from the script and any external resources, I then move to my own experiences and imagination to answer all of the questions found in Appendix 1. Don't be intimidated by the amount of questions. It might take a lot of focus and energy, but the results will be worth it. When answering these, I will write in my notebook in first person, as if I am the character, even down to the character's reaction to the question: 'Ugh why are we still talking about this. Yes, I'm blind in one eye, who cares, can we move on?!' or 'I am a little embarrassed about my love for my teacher, but cannot hide my feelings anymore.' Really have fun and go too far. Start getting to know the voice inside of their head. Start thinking like them. You will be amazed at what comes out of these questions, no matter how simple the answer is.

When preparing for a film, there was a scene where my character was talking to her boyfriend who was smoking. Somewhere in my character research I had ended up with a whole backstory about my character's uncle who had abused her as a child, and he was a smoker. That one piece of information, though it has nothing to do with the scene, changed my whole delivery and I had this fixation on the ashtray. My mind was busy and focused, not on the conversation, but on my character's own memories. The scene had a completely new focus and became so much more intense and interesting. I never discussed this with the director or the other actor. They didn't need to know my process. This was just mine and my character's secret.

Think of most of the conversations you have in a day. How often do you really mean what you say? If someone asks you if you're tired, because you look tired and only had four hours sleep, you might answer, 'not really' however what you mean is, 'I am exhausted!' You're annoyed at your partner because they've cancelled plans with you to go out with their friends; 'Is that ok?' they ask. 'Yeah, that's fine,' you answer, but really what you mean is, 'No, it's fucking not!' This is also known as subtext. This is my personal, final step after answering all of my character questions. Now that you have a good understanding of who your character is, go through every piece of dialogue in the script and write what your character is thinking next to the line.

For the most part you will find it very easy to relate to what your character is going through. In the case you find something that you cannot relate to, then get in contact with someone who can. I was playing a soldier's wife a few years ago. It was easy to imagine that my character would get worried and miss her husband, but I wanted to be more specific. I reached out to my cousin whose husband was in the army at the time. She told me it was more frustrating than scary having a partner in the army, because things changed all of the time and they couldn't make any plans. She didn't feel particularly worried either as she was quite used to it. This helped me build a more believable character rather than a stereotype, just by doing this extra research.

PLAYING REAL PEOPLE

If your character is based on a real person from the past, look for any books or articles online as well as shows or films which might give you more information. If someone else has already played the same character in a show or film, it may be wise to avoid watching their performance. You want your performance to be honest and original. If you see another person's version of your character and you like it, you may end up imitating them, rather than staying true to your own version of the character. It could also decrease your confidence if you feel the actor did such a good job that you couldn't possibly live up to the standard they had set. On the other hand, you could find it helpful if they did a bad job, to learn what not to do. Perhaps you could learn from their mistakes. If the character you are playing is no longer living but has relatives who are still alive, you may be able to get in touch with them and find out first-hand who this person really was. Please note that if you do decide to take this approach, speak to the director or producer first and be sure that contacting the family would be ok and they have given permission for the production to go ahead. You wouldn't want to appear insensitive or upset anyone.

If you are playing a character who is still living, do as much research as you can. Speak to your director and producers who may be able to introduce you to the person themselves. Only do this if your character is shown in a positive light and the real person is supportive of the story. If you are lucky enough to meet the real person that you are playing, make sure you are sensitive, respectful and don't push too hard with any of your questions if you feel like it might make them feel uncomfortable.

ACCENTS AND LANGUAGES

You may land a job where you are required to speak another language or with another accent. If you are highly skilled then great, but if you are still not 100 per cent confident in your own delivery then you could hire a voice or accent coach to help you. It's worth discussing at contracting stage, as this could be covered by production as part of your agreement. If it is not agreed to be covered by the production, then it could be a great investment to hire a coach for yourself. Unfortunately, if you perform with a poor accent the person who will receive the criticism is you. Doing a good job could secure you further roles with that accent and open you up to more work. It's not always the cheapest option but a good voice coach or language tutor will usually cost anything from around £35 to £125 per hour. You may need one to twelve lessons depending on your current skill level.

A cheaper option is a great language learning website called italki. com. Here you can do Skype calls with a language teacher from £5-£20 per hour and ask them to record your script in their accent. There are also some great, free tutorials on YouTube. Alternatively, you can reach out to anyone you know who is natively from the country that you need to do the accent from. Ask them to send you recordings of them reading the lines from the script for you to imitate. Being able to do accents well is a valuable skill for any actor. When you have downtime, broadening your accents and languages will open you up to more opportunities. If you do have additional accent or language skills, record yourself doing them and upload them to Spotlight 'voice clips' so casting directors can hear what you sound like.

LEARNING LINES

As mentioned before, knowing your lines is one of an actor's most important jobs. If you get a last-minute job there may be no time to do any character research, as learning the lines should always be your priority. Over time you will learn what works for you. Some actors are just blessed with a photographic memory, some prefer to run lines with people or some, like me, record the entire scenes to listen to. You may even be able to do some line runs with the other actors in the cast. If this is something you might be interested in, speak to the director who can arrange for you to meet up in person or you could run lines over the phone.

When preparing for a job it is also pretty useful to become familiar with the other characters' lines too. Certainly, the lines or actions that cue yours are very useful to know so that you don't interrupt their lines. It can also serve as a good place marker in case anyone accidently skips a few lines and you can pick up or improvise something convincing which might save the scene. Not only will the crew and director be grateful that you were able to keep on going, but so will the other actor, especially if it goes unnoticed. Just remember, you don't want to be obviously pre-empting the other actor's lines or mouthing along to them, which untrained actors have occasionally been known to do.

Learning one scene at a time is most useful. I recommend prioritising scenes that you are shooting first if possible, otherwise prioritise learning your most difficult scenes first. Scenes with a lot of action, a lot of characters, where you have the most lines or a large monologue could be the most challenging in terms of line learning. If it's a big and expensive scene to shoot with 100 extras and perhaps a few stunt guys, you don't want to be responsible for having to do a retake because you forgot a line. If you are pushed for time, leave the scenes with only a few lines to the night before so you are confident on the bigger scenes. Only do this if you are confident to do so.

Give yourself deadlines of when you will know your lines by so that you are in a good place. For feature films or TV shows, I like to be entirely off book a week before the shoot when possible. For shorts, I need to be off book a couple of days before. Once you are comfortably off book, you can play in the scene more. This is where acting gets really fun.

REHEARSALS

In theatre there is a long and in-depth rehearsal period. You can't restart the scene again if you mess up on stage, you have to nail it on the night. Besides, character work and scenes, entrances, exits and transitions all have to be planned and worked through with the actors. In film there is not so much pressure on the actor. The director, DOP and editor pick up most of the slack when it comes to the story telling. In television, especially in soaps, the work is so fast paced that there is no time for rehearsals. Film usually has a little more prep than television, depending on the director and the complexity of the scenes. In most cases only the key cast members will be called in for rehearsals and anyone with a minor role is expected to nail it on the day.

Be prepared for your first day of rehearsal so that you set off on the right foot with the other cast members and team. This is imperative for establishing the right kind of tone for the rest of the production. You don't want to be late or turn up on the wrong day or do anything that may hold up rehearsals and give you a bad reputation. At the same time, you want to keep things respectful and professional. Be warm and friendly at all times, do not brag, show off or be obnoxious. It can be very easy to fall into a subconscious 'role' of playing a diva when you are a little overwhelmed. Be conscious of your own behaviour. This is important, especially if you are playing the lead role. If this is the case, use your position to lead a positive, safe and enjoyable atmosphere for everyone to work in. Rehearsals can be a magical time for everyone and as long as you do the work and deliver what is asked of you all will be fine. Be aware that even if you make it to rehearsals, your place in the cast may still not be entirely safe. I know many an actor who has been 'replaced' during rehearsals, even the lead actors. It is much easier and cheaper to replace an actor at rehearsal stage, than when you have already shot half of the movie.

PERSONAL CARE

Before a shoot it is very important to make sure you are healthy, physically and mentally. Try to prepare your character work and lines as early as you can so that when it comes to the few days or nights before the shoot, you can relax. For most actors, jobs don't come along every day. When you do get a job it's important you are on top form and can enjoy it. After all of that hard work, you deserve it. Work equals work.

When you are on a roll, things can start happening and one job can lead on to another. You need to do your best to keep that momentum going. You don't want to push yourself too hard at the gym and end up with an injury. You don't want to eat too little and end up with low energy or passing out on set. Be good to yourself, this includes your mental health as well. Mediate, take breaks, listen to music, treat yourself to a massage, have a nice dinner, watch a movie, whatever it takes to make yourself feel good. Don't put too much pressure on yourself or let the job consume you. You might have to make some social sacrifices here and there, but you might not have to cancel important engagements entirely. Compromises can be made.

Rather than missing someone's wedding entirely, you could go for just a few hours. If you have to miss a friend's birthday party, then arrange a date to take them for dinner after the shoot. Not everyone will understand, but you have to be patient and know it's a compliment that they want you there for important moments in their lives. Make sure that if you cannot answer the phone or text messages from friends or family members during busy periods, you take the time to inform them you are busy and apologise, rather than ignoring them. An 'I am so busy filming' announcement on Facebook or Instagram will not suffice. If you are not great with texting then a voice note is a quick and easy, personal way of communicating. Do not ignore people or ever think you are too important to speak to them. All actors will come across quiet times and you don't want to burn bridges or abandon people who have been there for you all along. On the other hand, anyone who speaks about your career negatively or puts you down should not be tolerated. Surrounding yourself with positive and supporting people is very important for an actor. Your inner circle should consist of love and light. Though toxic energy can give us emotions to draw from in acting, these emotions are not helpful to use as actors in our day to day life or personal wellbeing.

CHAPTER 12

WORKING ON SET

Film sets can very busy places. Try not to get too distracted trying to make everyone your friend and just focus on the job at hand. The crew will put a lot of work into pre-production, weeks or even months of planning. Your department is the acting, so do not try to get involved with any of the other departments. The props department and wardrobe are not going to appreciate you telling them what you think would work better. Neither will the DOP want to discuss the difference between a RED Camera or Arri Alexa. To stay on the safe side, don't touch anything unless asked to and let any conversations come naturally, but do not distract the crew whilst they are working. Most film sets will be riddled with politics. Stay in your lane and focus on the work.

When you are shown to the green room/waiting area/dressing room/café – whatever the actor holding space may be – stay there until you wrap. If you need to go to the toilet, make a call, go to the shops, smoke a cigarette, then make sure that someone, preferably the first assistant director (1st AD), knows where you are at all times. You don't want to be the person who keeps the whole filmset waiting.

CALL SHEETS

The day before the shoot you will receive a call sheet. A call sheet is a document explaining the order of the day. This will include your 'call time' and the location you need to go to. Make sure you read this thoroughly, as your call location may be different to the unit base. The same call sheet is sent out to everyone in one document so everyone has the same information and there can be no excuses for crossed wires. It can be worrying if you have not received a call sheet by 7 p.m. the day before a shoot but it is very normal. don't worry. You should know roughly where you are going, or at least the postcode, a few days before the shoot but the final confirmed information may not be available until last minute. This is because a shoot requires so many factors to be in place like the weather, locations, people etc. Say you are shooting a scene on a sunny beach, but on the day of the shoot it is raining, the crew will probably have to shoot an indoor scene that day and the beach scene on a sunnier day. Or you are meant to shoot in a nightclub but the day before a shoot there was a real-life incident at the club, so now the police have shut off the scene. A little more extreme example, but it happens. If an actor in a minor role falls ill, they will probably be replaced. If a lead or 'name actor' falls ill, then the scheduled might be shuffled to make things 'work.'

Call sheets are very handy to refer to through the day in case you forget anyone's name. They should also include the scene which is being shot so you know which scene to prepare for. There will also be schedules available on set. Schedules will give you a breakdown of what is happening in each scene. If you can get hold of one of these, do. They are very useful and hold a lot more detailed information, like how many shots you are doing. Never share call sheets with anyone who is not involved on the production or post them online as they can include a lot of personal contact information.

WHAT TO BRING TO SET

It doesn't hurt to be over prepared when you go to set. In a dream world we all have our own condos and gourmet catering and we will be wrapped up in cotton wool and kept busy all day. This does happen, but not always. There's nothing worse than feeling grumpy on set because you feel a little neglected. A friend of mine once said people needed three things to feel happy; they need to be warm, fed and feel loved. Help yourself by packing a 'set bag.' Here is a list of things that I recommend to keep you feeling all of those things:

- Toothbrush, toothpaste and mints to stay minty fresh when getting in other another actor's space.
- Deodorant and wet wipes for freshening up between takes.
- A range of different coloured underwear and shapes in case your outfit requires it.
- A pair of comfortable shoes.
- Snacks, flask, water. These are mostly provided on set but it's good to have something you know you'll like.
- A couple of changes of clothes in case you're either kept in really hot or really cold conditions. For night shoots pack a blanket or water bottle.
- A paper fan in case you get too hot.
- Extra contact lenses/glasses in case you lose a lens or if you're feeling tired at the end of the day.
- Sunglasses for hot days, although you will probably be kept out of the sun to avoid tan lines.
- Laptop, book, headphones, iPad – whatever you need to keep yourself busy and entertained.
- A copy of your script – you can get some beautiful binders to protect your script and keep it safe.
- Tissues and antibacterial gel – you never know what the bathroom conditions will be like when shooting on location.
- Device chargers and a portable charger. When charging anything make sure it is away from production equipment. Firstly, so no one takes it. Secondly, never unplug anything on set. You can end up in a lot of trouble if you unplug the generator or a charging camera battery which could cost the production a lot of valuable time.

Being prepared will ensure you don't end up troubling the crew to borrow things and these little home comforts will also put you in a happy place so you can give a great performance and be vulnerable in the right kind of way. Most of the time the production and the crew will be very helpful and attentive.

WORKING WITH DIRECTORS

It is very important to maintain a good relationship with your director, but no two directors are the same. Each director will have a different approach to working. Some will just let you get on with it and you may not even get a single note on character or direction. This could be frustrating as actors like feedback and reassurance. Unfortunately, with this kind of director you won't get it. Not to worry though, that probably means they are happy with what you are doing. Believe in your own work and trust that everything is fine. You wouldn't have got the job in the first place if they didn't think you could do it.

Some directors might nit-pick at every single word and beat. You might get so many directions that it's suffocating and difficult to concentrate. You might think, why don't they just do the role themselves? As much as this is challenging, here you can actually end up creating an amazing performance without even realising it. It might not feel right to you but it could actually look amazing on camera. Always trust your director.

Other directors might end up feeling like a best buddie. These are my personal favourite. There's a mutual respect and understanding, you've got to know each other very well and your ambition and love of working together travels much further than just this project. You have fun on and off set and there is a real family vibe.

Whichever way your director works, you must trust them and their vision. If you do not understand a direction, do not be afraid to ask. Repeat the instructions back to them or mark it through so you are absolutely clear. Communication is a very important part of this relationship and pushing through a scene without understanding your notes or feedback could result in further retakes.

134

CREW MEMBERS AND WHAT THEY DO

If you have never worked on a filmset before or are still unfamiliar with some of the job roles, here is a brief overview of key crew members and how you might interact with them.

Producer: The producer takes the film from start to finish. Either from an idea or scripting stage, through to fundraising, hiring key personnel, contracting and distribution of the film. They are usually under a lot of pressure to stay inside the budget and when on set they are there to ensure that production have everything under control. Producers are great people to build relationships with. They have more pull on casting than a director.

Executive Producers: Investors or people who have contributed towards the project or helped get it made in some way. Sometimes they have no experience in film at all. Watch everyone panic and be on their best behaviour when they arrive on set.

Director: The creative visionary of the production and responsible for bringing the on-screen story to life by working closely with the cast and HODs (Heads of Department), from locations to cast, to wardrobe and everything in between. Communication is a key part of their role, leading the production and setting the tone of the work environment.

First Assistant Director (1st AD): The first assistant director is responsible for making sure that production sticks to the schedule. They oversee the cast and crew and ensure that everyone is focused on their work. If you have any issues on set, they can be a good person to talk to.

Second Assistant Director (2nd AD): The assistant of the 1st AD usually carries out any tasks delegated by them. They work very closely with the production team and are involved in creating the call sheets and making sure that everyone knows important information about what the shoot day entails.

Third Assistant Director (3rd AD): 3rd ADs are only required on larger scale sets to help with crowd scenes or complex shoots. They also assist the 1st AD or supervise the production assistants.

Director Of Photography (DOP)/Cinematography: Responsible for the look of the film. They work closely with the director and camera and lighting department. They make the decisions on lighting and framing of scenes.

Camera Operator: Sometimes the DOP might double up and do this role themselves, but otherwise this role will work closely with the DOP.

First Assistant Camera (1st AC)/ Focus Puller: The 1st AC is in charge of keeping the camera in focus when shooting.

Second Assistant Camera (2nd AC)/Clapper Loader: Operates the clapperboard and oversees the footage.

Data Wrangler: A very important job. They are responsible for uploading the footage from the camera to the hard drive. Never ask to plug your phone in near the data wrangler.

Line Manager: Manages the budget of the production and is responsible for the day to day physical aspects. A highly stressful and important job. A line manager once said to me, 'ever heard the term someone's neck is on the line? That's where the term comes from.'

Production Manager: A production manager supervises the personnel, schedule, budget and technology. They are responsible for making sure the production is on schedule and within budget.

Production Coordinator: The production coordinator is responsible for hiring crew, booking talent, renting equipment and organising the logistics.

Script Supervisor/Continuity: A script supervisor is in charge of making sure that the production stays on track with the script and keeps track of any changes. They keep notes on every shot and should be there to call you out if you, for example, pick up a prop with the wrong hand compared to previous scenes.

Stunt Coordinator: Stunt coordinators oversee and arrange the casting and performance of the stunts. Never try to convince the stunt director that you can do something. If a stunt performer has been hired to do it for you, they know best.

Stunt Performers: It takes years to join the stunt register and these performers are highly skilled. Respect what they do and never try to compete or try to give the stunt a go yourself. If production could have saved the money by letting you do your own stunt, they would have. Stunt performers don't come cheap and are only called in when needed.

Location Manager: Location managers are responsible for finding and securing locations for the production as well as coordinating any permits, the logistics and costs of travel.

Sound Recordist/Sound Mixer: Head of the sound department on set and responsible for all of sound including the choice of microphones. Also, the person who might attach a lavalier mic (body/clip/personal mic) to your chest when you have dialogue in a scene. You will also probably have a mic pack attached to your back pocket and a wire run through your clothes. Having a stranger put their hands under your clothes can be a little intrusive, but they will usually talk you through what they are doing. Keep in mind that it's probably more awkward for the recordist than for you. Making friendly conversation will make the process a little less uncomfortable. Don't forget, once you wrap for the day, or even if you want to leave set or to go the bathroom, find the sound recordist and let them detach the mic and pack for you.

Always be aware that once your mic pack is attached and turned on, everything you say could be heard. Now is not the time to have a little bitching session. Ever see that scene in Notting Hill where Julia Roberts is talking about Hugh Grant and he hears it through the headphones? You never know who is listening, so be careful what you say. If you need to run to the bathroom it's also a good idea to have the mic taken off, so that the recordist doesn't get a front row ticket to a sound show of you on the toilet.

Boom Operator: The boom operator is the guy who holds the fluffy thing on a stick above the actors' heads. It's not a real shooting day until the director has to call 'cut!' because the boom is in shot. They are responsible for the microphone placement and movement during the film.

Never think that you are more important than anyone else on set. Everyone is there to play their part, from extras to the cleaners. In most cases, aside from leading roles, actors are the most replaceable. There are so many talented people waiting in the wings, desperate to work. It will do you well to keep this as a state of mind. Treat everyone with the utmost respect, as you wish to be treated. If anyone is unkind to you don't worry, karma comes back around. If there are any persistent problems or big issues that need to be raised, then report it to your agent. If you don't have an agent representing you on this job, then report it to the production manager or 1ST AD.

PERFORMING INTIMATE SCENES

For most actors, at some stage in their lives they will be required to perform some kind of intimate scene. This could be anything from a hug, to a kiss to a sex scene. If you are working with an actor who you get on with then they can actually be quite fun. The other actor might not always be your cup of tea, but everyone has beauty in them. Find something that you do like about them and focus on that.

Whatever the scene entails, always make sure you are fully comfortable with the actions. If you are uncomfortable about something, then make sure you discuss it with your agent or the director in advance of the film day. If you do anything in front of the camera that you aren't happy with, the camera will probably see it and the scene won't come across well, that is unless you are meant to be repulsed by the other character. The shoot day is not the time to raise this concern and could end up making you look bad if you don't mention it sooner. You need to flag anything that you are uncomfortable with the moment that you read it in the script. Most of the time you will be told what the role will involve at the time of casting. If you audition for a role and know that it involves full frontal nudity, you are essentially saying 'yes, I am happy to do this.' If you are offered an audition for a role which will include nudity of any kind, you are completely in your right to ask what they have in mind and decide from there if you would like to do the audition or not.

There is also a personal side to filming intimate scenes. If you have a real-life partner, they may be a little uncomfortable with you performing such scenes. The best way to approach this is being open and honest. It can be, at times, part of an actor's job and so it's important they understand that it is purely professional. At the same time be sensitive and understand that it's a very unnatural part of a relationship and may have to be delt with delicately. A British actress once said that her husband always got upset about her performing sex scenes. That was until he was asked to do one with her, as it was only a small role with no lines. After that he realised how awkward and un-sexy it was and said that he would never get jealous again.

PROTECTING YOURSELF AND OTHERS
Since the Me Too movement there have been a lot of positive changes in the industry. During the Me Too movement many people, mainly women, spoke out against inappropriate sexual conduct in the workplace and this was particularly prominent within the

entertainment industry with many actresses coming forward. Most of the time intimate scenes are very consensual and professional, however, in an industry that is not easily regulated there are a lot of grey areas. It is best to approach the situation with extra caution and remember that the following apply:

• Nudity clauses should be negotiated at contracting phase. You should never have to prove that you can simulate sexual acts in an audition, neither on tape nor in person. If you become aware of anyone asking this of actors, please report them to the website that they have been advertising on, your agent and Equity, or any union protecting actors.

• Nudity or simulated sexual acts should always be agreed in advance of the shoot. If you are asked to do this on the day, then you have every right to refuse or have the discussion via your agent. Either way, you need to speak to your agent.

• If you suspect someone is being mistreated, discreetly discuss it with them or mention it to the production manager.

• Report any unacceptable behaviour to Equity or in cases of harassment or abuse then contact the police. Do not ignore this behaviour or try to take matters into your own hands.

In most businesses, if someone is behaving inappropriately then employees can go to HR who can deal with the person appropriately. Unfortunately, there is still no 'HR' in the entertainment industry but for now you can speak out and spread awareness to others so that we can call out anyone who is abusing their power.

Working on a filmset can be a wonderful experience but it is not always easy. As long as you are professional, kind to others and do a great job, you never know. This one job might lead on to another.

CHAPTER 13

STAYING PROACTIVE

It's easy to assume that once you wrap on a movie, you'll have to wait maybe six months until it's released. Then you can go to the fancy premiere, have your photos taken and use the footage and buzz of the film to get a new agent or catch the eyes of some casting directors and boom! Your acting career is sent into the stratosphere, never to return to out of work limbo again.

Sadly, in most cases that is not the way the cookie crumbles, especially when you're working independent films. The quickest I have known a movie to come out is eight months but on average you are looking at one to five years, but it could be longer. This includes short films and if a film is being submitted to film festivals, then you may even have to wait another year for release. Sadder still is that a lot of low budget films never even see the light of day. However, as you work your way up, the budgets will get bigger and there will be less chance of this happening.

Television is generally a lot faster and more certain but even then, for smaller roles there is always a chance your scene could get cut. So much of an actor's progression can depend on progress in their projects, but this is out of your control. Well, guess what, it doesn't have to be. In fact, there are many ways in which you can move your career forwards. In this chapter I will outline the ways you can keep busy and how there is always something to do. This will not only keep you positive mentally, but it will also create new opportunities and open doors.

SIDE JOB

If you had a million pounds, a great work ethic and were talented, I'm fairly sure you could become a 'name' pretty easily. You could do lots of acting courses, get a personal trainer, a makeup artist, a stylist and an assistant. You could get lots of fancy headshots, promotional and portrait shots. You could hire a writer and director and put on a one-person show for a week in a small studio theatre and invite agents and casting directors to come and see you. You could also hire another writer and director and create a low budget feature film for 100k. You could release it within 12 months and do lots of PR for yourself and the film. With the rest of that budget you could do two more films and keep it going until you were making money back or able to get more funding into future films. During this time, you would end up with a great showreel and catch the attention of casting directors and directors. I couldn't promise that you would become an A, B, or C lister, but with three leads in feature films and enough promotion, people would begin to know who you were. Yes, with money, hard work AND talent you can get things moving in this industry. But sadly, most of us don't have that kind of money and if you did, you would probably rather put it into property or somewhere low risk.

The point I'm making is that acting can be very expensive. Every year it's more headshots, equipment, events, training, memberships, unions, promotion, marketing, travel, rent, and so on. If you don't have some kind of financial backing and acting work, then you could end up living hand to mouth. You deserve more than this. Find an additional income stream which is flexible, something you enjoy and pays well. This way you can keep on investing in your career and lead a comfortable life. You don't have to be a 'struggling actor.' Going on holidays, eating out, living in a nice place and looking after yourself is something that everyone deserves. I spent many years of my life missing out on these things until I got my night job working in a casino. It was hard and it wasn't what I wanted to do but it enabled me to have a nice life and supported my acting career for many years. I owe a lot to that job and might not have stuck it out as an actor for so long without it.

Some of the best side jobs that I have come across include the following: personal trainer, fitness instructor, yoga teacher, massage therapist, casino croupier, beauty therapist, builder, construction worker, tree surgeon, teacher, estate agent, tutor, temp, makeup artist, photographer, camera man, brand ambassador, events manager, voiceover artist, driving instructor, just to name a few. Some of these careers will have some initial start-up costs and take some time but to have a backup plan and know how you are going to pay next month's rent, it's worth it.

FINDING AUDITIONS

This takes us back to the casting websites. Stay active and keep on submitting yourself where you can. You may not get consistent results, but if you are consistent then you will get results.

There are many ways of finding out what productions are shooting in the UK. Subscribing to production newsletters or magazines will let you know what is in pre-production, and you can then research on IMDB pro who is the assigned casting director. Be aware that not all of the information on IMDB is correct. Casting directors may still be attached to productions which fell through years ago and no one updated the information online. If you can't find the information online, you can message the production company or director directly to see who is casting.

If you watch a TV series and you think you would be perfect for it, get in touch with the director or producer on social media and start building a rapport. You may not get a reply straight away, but you know who they are and you might come across them again later. Many people also post castings on social media and it's a great way to get in direct contact with filmmakers.

NETWORKING

Ever noticed how the same directors and actors seem to work together time and time again? This is usually because they work together well on set but also have a great relationship off screen as well. For some filmmakers, when they start on a new project they might cast roles initially with people that they know before opening it up to casting. You could see this as frustrating, or you could use this to your advantage and grow your network of filmmakers.

It's very easy these days to get stuck behind your phone or computer but this is an industry of relationships. At some point you will need to get out there and get to know people in person. Emails and social media or even a Skype or Zoom call are fine initially, but there's nothing like the connection of meeting a person face to face. Attending film festivals, events, launches, workshops, screenings and premieres are all brilliant ways of meeting people organically. The term 'networking' can be daunting, even for actors, but if you look at it as 'making friends' then it makes it a whole lot easier.

For some people networking comes very easily. If you are not one of those people, then do some research into how you can improve your networking skills. When networking, there can be a fine line between being confident and arrogant. Make sure the conversation is going both ways. Concentrate on them and ask questions. This isn't about looking for what you can get out of someone, everyone is interesting in some way, you just have to listen. Other people may find it difficult talking about themselves. If this is something that you struggle with perhaps practice introducing yourself in a couple of lines. What makes you different? What might people find memorable? Still not sure? Ask some acting friends and see what they say. Believe in yourself and your work but at the same time you must never lie. People are very good at smelling bullshit and you don't want to get off on the wrong foot or leave a bad impression by lying or making out that you have done something that you haven't. Try to focus on what you have already achieved rather than roles that you are up for. A friend of mine used to go around telling people that she had ten feature films in development that she was attached to. Technically it was true, but everyone in the business who she spoke to knew the likelihood of all ten of those films getting off the ground was very small, so she came across a little naive.

Networking can come in the strangest of places. Even a friend's birthday party or a distant relative's wedding, you never know who you're going to meet. Do you need business cards? I really think this is personal preference these days. I used leave festivals with hundreds of business cards. I would then shove them in a pile and two years later realise that I had done nothing with them and then throw them in the bin. These days I would prefer to take someone's Instagram details or phone number to a business card, but they are still useful to have.

SOCIAL MEDIA

Some people love it, some people hate it, but social media has taken over the world and sometimes it's better to go with the tide rather than fight against it. If you are an actor and you are actively trying to get more work, but you are not utilising social media, I seriously think you are missing a trick. Not only is it networking heaven and a platform for you to showcase your work, but it is also free! The minimum I think every actor should be on is Instagram, Twitter and Facebook. Posting doesn't have to be time consuming, but it should be consistent. You can link your accounts together so that when you post on one platform, it automatically shares the same post to the others. Treat your social media pages like your casting websites; professional, clean and consistent. The fun thing about social media is that you can be creative and showcase your talents and personality. You can essentially do your own marketing for free. If you still don't have a clue, watch some YouTube videos on how to get set up.

What's in a name? Well, everything if you want people to search for you. If you have a stage name, make sure you use that on everything work related, including your business social media. Your stage name is essentially your company name, so you need to make sure it is everywhere. This will also avoid mishaps when it comes to production credits. Your work email address should also include your acting name. You wouldn't want to miss out on a job just because someone wasn't sure if they had your correct email address.

Profile and cover photos should be professional photos where possible. You don't have to use your headshots as they can be a little neutral and don't always say much about your personality. This a perfect place to use images from creative photoshoots. Anywhere you can, write a short biography, be as creative as you like but make sure you include that you are an actor.

Facebook

I know some people aren't keen on using Facebook for personal reasons but what I'm talking about is setting up a profile for work use only. Despite not spending much time on Facebook, I actually have two accounts. One is personal and the other is for business and I do my best to keep them separate. Why? Because I don't want my work acquaintances seeing photos of me on Christmas day or hanging out with family. The real me can be quite different to the business me and I prefer to keep them separate online. I also don't want my friends or family seeing promotional photos of my in my underwear or having to read another post every time I have a new voiceover job and am promoting that I am available in case more work comes up. Sometimes there will be crossovers if I have something very exciting happening, but most of the time it's pretty separate. You can also set up a Facebook Page for yourself as an actor. It's a little more one sided, like a newsletter where the audience can see your posts. Pages give the users a bit more choice. If my friends and family are interested in my work, they can like my page. If they are not interested, they don't have to and it's really not a problem.

Whatever you do, do not use your Facebook to vent or slag people off. Passive aggressive posts can also be off putting. People will want to look at your posts because they put them in a good mood. If you have a strong cause you want to promote, using your platform to spread awareness for that is great too. but using your platform to moan is unlikely to grow followers, if that is what you are looking to do.

Instagram

A favourite amongst creatives as it's the most visual of all the platforms, hence why it's so popular amongst the entertainment industry and it's really easy to connect with other people. Pay attention to how your profile page looks and how all of your images look together. The most successful profiles on Instagram have a very clean and unified look with a theme throughout. Stories are another great way to share what you've been up to, almost like your own reality TV show. Instagram is quite a competitive place these days and algorithms, which decide what photos are shown at the top of feeds, change all of the time. It doesn't hurt to be in touch with the basics of how these things work, generally the more you interact with other people and use the platform, the better your posts will do.

Tip: Do not buy followers. It is very obvious that your followers are fake when you have 20k followers but get 20 likes on a post. There are also websites that can calculate the percentage of your followers that are fake. Anyone can put your details in and expose you for buying followers. This could get you into an embarrassing situation or could result in a ban from your account. A good quality, interactive, smaller following is much more impressive than a low quality, high following.

Twitter: This is worth having as a lot of jobs get posted here. It's also very easy to interact within the industry. You do have to be cautious about what you are liking, as this information gets pinned to your account. An innocent passing comment meant in jest can be seen years later and has got some celebrities in serious trouble.

LinkedIn: Less obvious but definitely worth having. A more professional way of approaching people and there are all sorts of interesting opportunities to be found.

Pinterest: Not many people realise that Pinterest is actually a search engine for images and a very powerful one at that. You can upload photos and use hashtags to send traffic to your images. Each image can also have a website link attached so if anyone clicks on your image you can send them wherever you would like more views. Your personal website, IMDB, Facebook or Instagram pages are useful places to send your audience.

YouTube And Vimeo: Having both of these channels is useful as on occasion a CD might specifically ask you to upload a self-tape to one of these sites. Whenever you have a new showreel, delete your old one from both of these sites and upload your new one. It can be a little tedious but it's useful for embedding showreels onto a website and you may even get 'traffic' from people looking for actors.

'Hash Tags': If you are not utilising hashtags then you are missing a trick. On all platforms you can use hashtags to bring people to your post who search for that word. Google is now also picking up these hashtags to show in their search pages. For every post you put out, add three to eight hashtags at the end which appropriately outline you and what you are posting about, for example, #mauritianactress #stagecombatperformer #britishactor. Using your name as a hashtag will tell Google to show this video when people search for you, making your online presence stronger.

LEARN NEW SKILLS
Skills can make you memorable and valuable if not many other actors can do what you can. The brilliant thing about skills is that most of them can be learnt. If you are quite athletic then do some

stage combat courses, learn a martial art or keep in practice with any sports you were good at in school. You could learn a language or practice accents. I used to listen to an American accent audio book whilst I was driving and practice on my way to work. You don't always have to be an expert in your skill, you just need to be able to do enough to convince the audition panel and the audience. Driving is obvious, but if you don't have it, it's also a great life skill and seems to come up a lot. For more inspiration visit the skills section on Spotlight and write down ten new skills that you think would come up for your cast type. Now do some research and find out which of these skills would be easy, affordable and accessible for you to train in. Once you have your top two skills, get training. You can come back to your list once you are at a good level with these skills and build up from there.

VOICEOVER

Voiceover work can be extremely lucrative, but it is by no means easy. These days you don't have to have a top voiceover agent to get work, you can find it yourself. Going into voiceover work as a trained actor gives you an immediate advantage because of the voice skills and character skills you would have already learnt. However, there is a lot to learn especially if you are planning on starting up your own home recording studio.

The basic set up is pretty simple. You just need a laptop, a good microphone, some recording/editing equipment and your unique voice talent. I use a Macbook Pro, Adobe Audition, NT2A Rode mic and Scarlett 2i2 interface, which, minus the laptop, cost around £400 to set up plus around £20 a month for Adobe Audition, but you can spend as much or as little as you like. Price doesn't necessarily mean better quality but avoid USB mics where possible. The quality won't be as good, and your recording quality needs to be of a certain standard as the competition from other voiceover artists is so high. Once you have bought your equipment and soundproofed your studio space, you will need to learn how to use it all. You can find a lot of information online and there are many great online courses which will teach you everything you need to know.

You will also need a great website. You don't have to spend loads on a developer either. It took a while, but I created my voiceover website myself www.jadeashavoiceovers.com using wix.com. Most importantly you will need clients. Yes, lovely people that want to pay you for your wonderful talent. You can do this by signing up to pay to play sites, where you pay a monthly fee to access auditions, or you can directly email production companies and casting directors yourself. This is only skimming the surface. It takes real hard work and dedication to become a successful voiceover artist, like any business, but the rewards in doing a job that you love are more than worth it and it definitely fills that acting hole.

PODCASTS

Apparently, everyone these days has a podcast, but how many people out of everyone you know actually does have their own podcast? Probably not that many. Not only is it a great marketing tool for yourself but if you have guests on your show, it can be great for other people too. They are very cheap to run, depending on the platform that you go with, around £12 per month. They don't have to be about acting either. There are successful podcasts about everything you can think of. From knitting to business, to parents writing porn books (you know the one.) You could do a fiction podcast and get writers to submit their work and perform it with a group of actors. That would be a great promotion for yourselves and the writers, and who knows who could hear it. Having produced two successful podcasts Acting With Asha and No Drama I have also compiled a free 10 Steps to Creating A Successful Podcast in Appendix 5. If you are already a voiceover artist and have the equipment, then you already have everything you need to start a podcast.

JOIN TABLE READ GROUPS

Table reads are a great way for writers to try out new material. It usually consists of a group of actors reading in one or a few different roles, whilst the writer listens to the script being read out loud and takes notes. Sometimes there are industry professionals invited, who might be interested in producing the material. Sometimes there is a director involved if the read through is staged. This is not only a great networking opportunity and a chance for you to practice your skills, but you could end up cast in one of the roles. There are many table read groups in London but if there isn't one in your area or you already have a group of actors who might be interested, you could set up your own. During lockdown a few actor friends of mine set up a WhatsApp group and we had several Zoom read throughs of our own work which felt really productive.

WRITE YOUR OWN MATERIAL

Becoming a writer is a whole new skill in itself but it will elevate you as an actor in many unexpected ways. Not only will you have the skills to write your own work, but you will have a better understanding of when a script is good and when a script is not so good. Besides character development and an unexpected twist, there are many other intricacies which sets aside a good script from a great script. There are many books and courses and in person and online masterclasses and seminars that are easily accessible and either free or very cheap. Or, if you would rather focus on the acting, then you could find a new writer who is looking for some experience and collaborate or hire them to work on a script with you. If you do go down this route, make sure you both sign an agreement outlining who owns the rights and if there will be a profit share if the script is sold or a production makes a profit.

Just because you are not acting, it does not mean that you are not working on your acting career. Most successful entrepreneurs will have multiple businesses. You are an actorpreneur. It's time to start thinking like one.

CHAPTER 14

MAKING YOUR OWN WORK

Actors creating their own work is by no means a new thing, but it is certainly more popular now that filmmaking has become much more accessible. Shooting an entire feature film will still cost you an arm and a leg, and you would need some kind of investment to pay the cast, crew, locations and at the minimum keep everyone fed and watered. However, you don't have to make full length feature films. There are many other different formats, which are much easier on a budget. You could create your own showreel scenes, short films, web series or theatre shows. These are all possible to achieve with a lot of hard work and a very modest budget. Creating your own work will not only give you credits, new strings to your bow, footage and some kudos, it will give you some control of your career which will do wonders for you self-confidence and mental health.

WORK WITH WHAT YOU HAVE

As actors, we will most likely want to create something which has a fast turnaround time. Therefore, whatever you decide to do has to be cheap/low budget, very simple and require a minimum amount of people to be involved. Before you start writing your project, consider what and who you have available to you. Does a friend of yours work at a theatre and you can use the space for a low rate or for free? Could you use your own home as a location? Cars? Nightclubs? Remember, there will be other unavoidable costs later on so aiming to spend nothing on locations will set you off on the right foot. In 2017 I wrote and produced a short film called The Contract. I was living in a one-bedroom flat at the time, so set the entire film there.

STORY

When deciding what your script is going to be about choose a subject that is important to you and has a powerful message. You want to be able to move people, whether it's to make them angry, laugh or cry. It's all well and good choosing an action scene just because you want to look badass and hold a gun, but there has to be a strong reason behind it and an interesting story. Do not take your audience for granted. They will see through self-indulgence. Whatever you choose to make your script about, make sure you really love and believe in the idea. You could be working on it for a long time, years even. There will be lots of hurdles to overcome so your need to finish the project has to be strong enough to push it through the hard times.

SCRIPT

As mentioned in the last chapter, there is a lot to learn when it comes to writing but you can find most of the information you need online. Perseverance is key. How do you write? One word at time. The key thing is to start writing and keep going until you finish it. Most people who start writing something, never finish it. So, if you can make it to the end of a script, you are already head and shoulders above the rest. What if it's terrible? Everyone's first draft is terrible, even famous writers will tell you that. Good writing is rewriting. Editing draft after draft until you trim the fluff and are left with a clear and concise script. Take advantage of table read groups or hire/collaborate with other writers. Still need inspiration? Write about something that you experienced or is very important to you. If you don't fancy writing yourself why not use a story or characters which are in public domain (no one owns the rights to). It's best to do some thorough research on this. Shakespeare's plays, for example, are in public domain so are free for you to use and perform without permission needed.

BUDGET

Once you have a script you are happy with, you will need to write a budget. This can be tricky on your first production. If you want to put on a one-person theatre show, make sure props and costumes can be borrowed or bought cheaply. Your main costs will be on the venue, marketing, technical engineer and front of house staff.

For film you need to break down how many people you need involved. This includes cast and crew. How much will you need to cover their food and travel expenses at the very minimum? If you have a bigger budget, for a guideline on how much cast rates are look on the Equity website and for crew, BECTU, although for lower budget you could get away with minimum wage or some people may collaborate if it's a passion project.

You also need to consider whether you will need to cover travel expenses, accommodation, hard drives (back up the footage at least twice) props/costumes, lighting, camera hire, insurance, editing, sound, music, colour grading, film festival fees, screening costs, poster design and marketing.

Of course, as actors making our own work many of these corners can be cut and you will find that you end up doing most of these things yourself. However you plan your budget, always allow for an extra 20 per cent contingency. Filmmaking is very unpredictable, after all.

FINANCING

Some would argue this is the most difficult hurdle in the filmmaking process. In most cases you will need some source of finance to get your production off the ground. There are several ways of doing this. Bear in mind that if you are new to filmmaking the likelihood of you making any return will be quite slim so until you have made a couple of productions, do not borrow large amounts that you will be expected to pay off.

Self-Funding

Money is indeed power, especially in filmmaking. If you can invest yourself then great, it will give you creative control over all aspects of the production and no one to answer to.

Crowd Funding

A popular way of raising finance, usually through an online platform where you can set a target amount of money to raise and backers will essentially 'gift' you money, in exchange for rewards which you set out yourself. Having run two successful campaigns and two unsuccessful campaigns, I would say the following:

• Keep your goal realistic, in most cases you can always keep raising money after you hit your goal.

• You have to be extremely proactive messaging people and following up, even just asking them to share the campaign if they cannot afford to financially support you. It needs to be a full-time job.

• Be prepared to contribute yourself to get it off of the ground. There's nothing more unappealing than a project that is only three per cent funded. Why should other people invest in you if you cannot invest in yourself?

• Be extremely thankful and loud about being thankful. People love to be praised and if you do it publicly, it will most likely push someone else to get involved.

• People love to back a winning horse. The hardest part will be the beginning but once you have lots of support behind the project the energy will take you over the finish line.

• Make sure the 'rewards' you are promising people are not going to eat into your budget or be too time consuming to fulfil. Giving away signed props/scripts/credits/thank you dinners/phone calls/

set visits are all really cool rewards and easy to deliver.

Investors
If you do have any private investors there are government schemes like the Enterprise Investment Scheme (EIS) and the Seed Enterprise Investment Scheme (SEIS) which offer great tax return incentives. When approaching investors, you will have to have an in-depth breakdown of the budget and 'exit strategy' or way that you will be able to earn their money back and make a profit. When working with investors they will usually be given an executive producer credit but also have an input on the financial and creative decisions. If you go down this route, you must make sure there are contracts in place, and you are in control of the money before preproduction starts.

Funding
There are many different funding bodies who are there to finance new filmmakers. When applying for funding there is usually a lot of competition and paperwork to fill out. There might also be guidelines which you have to adhere to in order to be eligible for the funding.

DIRECTORS AND PRODUCERS
Are you going to work with directors and producers or are you going to do it all yourself? If your goal is to come up with a piece that showcases your acting, then working with a director would be a smart move. Filmmaking is stressful at the best of times so having someone to take the pressure off will feel like a god send. It will also allow you to focus on the acting and allow for a stronger performance. If you didn't want to produce the entire thing yourself, you could find someone to co-produce with you. Some people will not finance you unless you have a director attached and some directors will not attach themselves to your project until you have finance in place. The earlier you bring on the directors and producers the better. Productions usually have a snowballing effect. As soon as you attach people things start moving really fast and they will also bring their own resources in. Ride that momentum as hard as

you can. Once it stops it can be very difficult to get going again.

CASTING

90 per cent of directing is casting. A famous notion which describes that if a film is cast well, and according to the director's vision, it will make for a far better end result. This speaks volumes about why casting is so important. When posting your castings, be as thorough about what is expected from the actors, for example, driving, romance, fight scene. If you are using a casting venue, choose one that has an easy location to get to and accessible times for actors. If requesting self-tapes be clear how the actors need to submit themselves. You could also do a Skype audition which would save costs on the venue. For low/no budget productions you can submit breakdowns for free on Mandy.com or if your budget is good and you can pay Equity minimum rates then you can advertise on Spotlight.com. I'm often surprised at how many actors forget what it's like to be an actor as soon as they move to production. In whatever role you are in, always be organised, transparent, respectful and professional at all times. Exactly how you would hope to be treated.

CREWING

There are many job roles required for filming but on smaller productions I would recommend that you hire a director, DOP, camera assistant, sound engineer, gaffer, production manager, hair/makeup and a runner. This is a bare minimum and that is eight people. This is assuming you will be providing your own clothes, props, locations and doing the casting yourself. If you are shooting a single scene you could just get away with a camera person and sound. There are several places you can find crew but for low budget work I would usually go to Mandy.com. Here be as transparent as possible as to what the job role is, if equipment is required, the pay and what type of production you are making. When hiring crew, I recommend meeting them in person or holding a Skype interview. Building some kind of rapport and checking that they will bring a good energy to set.

CONTRACTS AND RELEASE FORMS

If you hire a production manager, they will be in charge of organising the contracts, however you as the producer will be held accountable so you need to make sure you oversee the information and that everyone has signed them. The contracts should be clear, and you should cover yourself as much as possible. Though nothing comes close to a lawyer writing a contract, there are some basic templates that you can use online. It is vital that you ask anyone who is appearing on the screen to sign a release form. This gives you permission to use their image. Without this they could decide they don't want you to use their footage anymore and will have the right to stop you using material with them in. It is also a good idea to get location contracts so that there are no issues on the day of filming. Make sure you keep all of your contracts safe and on file. If you do end up selling your project it may be on the terms that you can provide this information.

PRE-PRODUCTION

A huge part of filmmaking is problem solving. During your pre-production meetings make sure that the shoot is planned in as much detail as possible. Create contingencies and back up plans for all situations. Account for weather changes, safety, noise, delays, batteries going flat, backing up footage, changing locations, camera set ups, comfortable green rooms and catering areas for cast and crew. Arrange for rehearsals with key cast members so everyone knows what they are doing and can nail their scenes on the day. Make sure the schedules and call sheets are well thought out and that everyone is aware of what they are doing.

PRODUCTION

I wish I could give you some more specific information here, but each production faces its own challenges and that would be another book in itself. All I can say is that production can be an incredibly stressful time for everyone but remember why you are doing it and always be grateful and respectful to all of those on set. As a leading person in the production people will look to you for guidance and answers. It can be a little overwhelming at times but keep your cool and it will all work out in the end. At the end of the day it's only a film and your own and your cast and crew's health and safety should always come first.

POST-PRODUCTION

Getting a film through to post-production is a massive achievement. Here might seem like a good place to rest and recover. It's not. Too many people let that momentum drop but you need to be the driving force which sees it through to completion. Most issues I have found in post-production have been due to schedule clashes or getting hold of people. Make sure you have copies and backups of all of the footage the day that you wrap or the very next day. Always be in possession of the footage, it is months or even years of your hard work. Do not put that responsibility on anyone else.

You should already have an editor lined up and ready to go. The editor will put together the first assembly or 'rough cut' and after that you or the director can join them for sessions or if you are working remotely then you can send them notes. It might take a few more passes but eventually you will end up with a 'Picture Lock' which is the final edit. The Picture Lock can then be sent out simultaneously to your sound designer and a separate colourist for grading. Once sound and colour are completed, the files should be sent back to the editor to slot them all together, including the credits and titles. Of course, depending on the project and how skilled you are, you could just do all of this work yourself but obviously it's always good to have an additional perspective.

Now you have your final file, whatever that format is. These days you are most likely looking at a 1080p (Full HD) or 4k sized file. Another surprise cost, if you are planning on showing your production in the cinema is a DCP (Digital Cinema Package) which will cost anything from £100+ for a short or £300+ for a feature.

Tip: The first edit is not the final product. Most likely far from it. Colour, music and much more editing can transform a film. I personally have a habit of crying every time I watch my footage back and getting incredibly upset about how I let everyone down. The next day I will watch the footage again and realise that actually it wasn't as bad as I thought. It is extremely hard acting and producing a project. Do not let your ego get in the way and let you down. All you need is a bit of perspective.

FILM FESTIVALS

If you do decide to send your project to film festivals, you will need a healthy budget to submit your project. Film festivals are not just for films either. There are festivals for just about anything: web series, films shot on camera phones, trailers, documentaries. Film Freeway is my favourite site for submitting to film festivals. You just upload your file along with all of the promotional materials and information about the filmmakers. Add your selected festivals to a basket, pay and off they go. It couldn't be easier. Some film festivals such as Cannes and the BFI London Film Festival will only accept submissions through their websites, so you have to do a little more research.

PROMOTION

Once your film is complete it's time to come up with a strategy so that people know about it. Are you having a screening? Are you going to put it straight online? Try to sell it? Come up with an in-depth strategy as to how you want to deliver your project to the world. Images and trailers of the film pre-release can build up a lot of hype and make people excited about your project. Premieres are the ultimate hype and you find some good deals on cinemas if you look around and book their off-peak time slots. There's a brilliant company called Our Screen who will screen your film once you have sold X amount of tickets in mainstream cinemas. Again, you may have to really hustle if you are selling tickets, but it is worth it. This is also the perfect opportunity to offer casting directors and agents complimentary tickets. Even if they can't make the screening, they will most likely be impressed with your proactivity. You could then send them a private link for them to watch your project in their own time.

This is just a very brief overview of what it takes to produce your own work. Have you got a story that just won't leave you alone? What would you like to share with the world or change about it? Do not be intimidated or afraid. You can do anything if you put your mind to it. You just need to give yourself the chance.

CHAPTER 15

PREMIERES, EVENTS AND PR

Although the red carpets, fancy clothes and photoshoots shouldn't be the reason you become an actor, it can become a big part of the job. Some producers will even write into their actors' contracts that they must attend the premiere and X amount of screenings and share X amount of posts about the film. Some actors have said sometimes they spend more time promoting the film then they did shooting it. There's no wrong or right way to show up to a screening and watch a movie, but there are ways you can make the most of it, especially when you are an up and coming actor. In this final chapter I would like to share some information I wish I had known about attending events and premieres, and how to do your own PR work.

SCREENINGS

Cast and Crew Screenings
There is a huge difference between a screening and a premiere. Screenings are usually day or evening events and you should dress smart/casual to these events. They can include the cast and crew screening, which is usually the first time that everyone who has worked on the production, whether film or TV, gets to see it. TV shows also sometimes hold premieres where they might show one or two of the episodes, as they are often shorter than feature films.

At a cast and crew screening everyone will usually know each other. Having worked together for a long time but maybe not seen each other in months or even years, this could be a big reunion and very relaxed. Expect lots of laughter and heckling from in jokes and a really fun atmosphere (unless everyone hates the film). This is a great opportunity to network and make some contacts by asking everyone about their experience and contribution to the film. This is not a great place to over dress and spend ages taking selfies as you could come across a little desperate.

Private Screenings and Film Festivals
These are usually smart casual events and will include invited professionals from the industry. They are another place to network and ask people about their connection to the film.

General Screenings
These are usually very relaxed and casual. They will be full of members of the public who might get a bit scared if you try to talk to them, as it's not a professional event. Though everyone else may be casual, smart casual is great because you are an actor and always want to try and look a little bit fabulous.

Tip: When attending any kind of industry screening or premiere, warn your guest that it's etiquette to sit through the credits at the end of the film. Their confused faces will be that little less excited, but it will save you from some funny looks if you get up too early.

ATTENDING PREMIERES
If you have been invited to a premiere, you are a very lucky chosen one. There is, of course, the dilemma of what to wear. By all means get your hair and makeup done and buy a new outfit, just remember to be respectful that this is the cast and crew's big moment. There is a little unsaid etiquette that unless advised otherwise, you should not dress up in a full-length gown or tuxedo unless you were a part of the cast or crew. It's sort of like turning up to someone else's wedding in a wedding dress. By all means be smart and look great

but not too over the top.

You will most likely be given some kind of invitation. Do not lose this as they may not let you in without it. With premieres, times are usually very precise due to the expense of running such a big venue, so factor in arriving early so that you don't have to rush. The cast will usually arrive early so they can spend time on the red carpet doing photos and giving interviews. Eat and drink before you go to a premiere because bizarrely the bar and snack counter is not always open. Sometimes there will be bottles of water, goodie bags, sweets or popcorn waiting for you at your seat but sadly sometimes there is not.

When you arrive at a premiere there is usually someone with a clipboard full of photos of the key cast, crew and any famous attendees. This list lets the press know who they should be taking photos of. If you are not on the list, the press most likely will not take photos of you. If you are feeling super gutsy then you could confidently walk up to the press board, pose and smile and maybe they will take photos of you. Be warned this could be an awkward and embarrassing risk if everyone ignores you. A safer option would be to wait until a section of the press board is free, or until after the film, and ask someone to take a couple of photos of you then. It's also a great opportunity to network and if you speak to the right people you could be invited to the after party.

YOUR PREMIERE

Attending a premiere of a movie that you acted in, is certainly something to be proud of. It's more than just a screening. It's a celebration. A symbol that all of your hard work and perseverance has paid off. It can feel like your wedding day in many ways and you should make the most of it. Sadly, even at your own premiere you may only take one person so you should choose wisely. It can be extremely overwhelming, especially when everyone wants to talk to you and you're probably wearing something quite uncomfortable. I learnt that my sister, Suki, is the perfect premiere guest as she's great at almost doubling as a PA. She'll hold my bag, make sure I've had a drink and check that I'm not having any makeup or wardrobe malfunctions. I'm not sure what I would have done without her. So, when confused between who to invite, consider who will be a great Suki.

Before the premiere there is much to consider including what to wear, but it's not a dilemma that you have to face alone. Stylists can be the voice of reason you need. Yes, they can be pricey but for the money you spend on one dress that you will only wear once, they can arrange for you to borrow a whole designer outfit including jewellery, shoes and accessories. A stylist will already have great relationships with brands and PR companies. They will arrange for you to go and try on loads of beautiful and expensive outfits that you would never see on the high street. I was lucky enough to work with the extraordinary Mekel Bailey on my first premiere and on other productions since.

Hair and makeup are also very important when it comes to premieres. A makeup artist friend of mine actually specialises in doing premiere makeup for famous male actors –lucky thing. So, the guys do need to think about these things too. For smaller events I will work with someone who can do both hair and makeup but for bigger events I will hire individual hair and makeup artists for my glam team. Indeed, all of this does add up and, in the end, I think I spent around £700 on beauty and styling for one event. Certainly not something that I could afford every week. Over time, and because I was able to get such great photos from this event, I started to build my own relationships with different designers and brands, who I emailed or met via Instagram. For bigger events, definitely work with a stylist. In any case, you want to pre-plan your whole look in as much time as possible so that there are no last-minute panics on the day.

Having a backup outfit isn't a bad shout either. Any items that are loaned to you by the stylist, designer or agency should be looked after and returned immediately and in perfect condition. So, make sure you look after them otherwise they won't want to work with you again in the future. Whenever you get lent or gifted anything, a thank you card, small gift and social media shout out will go a long way and potentially lead to more freebies.

If possible, try and get ready in a hotel room near the premiere location so there is less time between your makeup being applied and walking the red carpet. Otherwise arrive in a car/taxi allowing plenty of time for traffic as premieres usually welcome arrivals from 5.30/6 p.m., right in the middle of rush hour.

Be aware that from the moment you step in front of the photographers, they are taking photos of you the whole time. Keep your hands relaxed, your posture straight and keep smiling and posing until they stop. No adjusting underwear and keep your face relaxed and smiling.

Stay hydrated and if there is alcohol on offer don't have too much. There may be some great networking opportunities throughout the night and though you should enjoy yourself, all eyes will be on you so try to be on best behaviour. That is until you get to the after party. The day after the premiere press photos should already be available online so you will be able to update your IMDB and social medias immediately, but these photos should not be used for casting websites.

FILM FESTIVALS

There are hundreds of film festivals around the world. They can be great networking opportunities and often, as an industry professional you can often get industry accreditation to watch the films for free. Be aware that these are film markets and so most beneficial for people who are buying or selling movies. Never the less they can be a really fun experience, although if you don't have a film at the festival or are not already invited to events and parties then it can be a bit of a hustle.

EVENTS

Events can range from award ceremonies to product launches. You may find you are invited to these things from time to time but treat them as an extracurricular. These can be great opportunities to meet people from other industries, get a few photos and freebies and have a fun night. It's easy to get swept away by the glamour of it all but you have to remember this is not the goal, the work is. Never mess up a job or miss an audition because you went out the night before. Always make an effort to look good and avoid drinking too much. As fun as it is, if you get too merry that one time, the invitations may dry up all together.

PR

If you can afford a PR company when you have notable work coming out, take advantage of this opportunity and start building your profile. A PR company will help you to gain press coverage and build a good reputation in the media, but with a hefty price tag. Starting at £500 per month for at least three months at the lower end of the spectrum, it can be a big expense. You can very easily do your own PR when you're starting out by organising interviews in newspapers, radio shows, podcasts and blogs. Sometimes all it takes is a few emails or direct messages to and fro and you could have a full spread in your local newspaper. You have to remember that if your work does well and has exposure then it benefits your reputation well. This extra bit of effort could lead on to more work or the producers being so pleased with your support they decide to hire you again for their next project. Like all things, this is a numbers game. Don't be disheartened if you send five emails and don't hear anything back. Send one hundred messages and you will get a response. Hard work always pays off.

Attending events and premieres can give you some great content for your social media and building your online presence. You can also make some great industry connections, but don't get too swept up in it and always remember that the work comes first.

CHAPTER 16

THAT'S A WRAP

To survive in this industry, you have to build emotional strength to endure all that it will throw at you. Love yourself and be brave enough to spend your life doing what you love doing. Trust your own instincts and find whatever works for you. I do not expect you to agree with my approach or ideas, they are only what has worked for me and what I wish someone had told when I was starting out.

I do hope what I have shared may shed some light on some areas of the industry you have not yet explored and that you will take my experiences and use them to make informed decisions, whenever you approach something new. If you read this book because your passion for the industry was burning out, I hope this book has helped relight that flame or at least created a spark. I hope that it might help you with any decisions you were stuck on, or perhaps inspire you to create your own work, if before you didn't know where to start. I hope that if acting is in your heart but earning money is in your head, you don't feel like you have to choose between the two. You can do both.

Remember all of the applause, good reviews and awards in the world will not make you happy if you are not happy within yourself. I do recommend counselling to everyone, especially if you are dealing with difficult issues.

In an industry where so many people are talkers, I hope you take courage to be a doer. Deliver on those promises to yourself. The fact you have taken time to read this book already shows your commitment. We know that certain things are not in your control but hopefully now you see some things can be. I am a great believer that this is our one chance at life and if you want something then you have to be willing to put the work in to get it.

You might be afraid that many of the actions you can take in this book require a lot of attention from people who may judge you. So what? Is their judgement going to pay your bills? Give you the life that you've always wanted? Who cares? It is better to be talked about than not talked about. If someone is talking about you, you must be doing something right. Being an actor can be difficult but only because it is one of the greatest jobs on earth. If it was easy everyone would be doing it, and nothing worth having ever came easy.

Though you must push your boundaries and step out of your comfort zone, always put your health, happiness, friends and family first. There is no point in climbing to the top of the mountain if you are going to have no one to share the view with. Neither is burning yourself out and suffering physically or mentally. Be kind to yourself and find the simple pleasures that ground you and make you happy, whether it be a walk in the park, a warm bubble bath or watching your favourite movie in bed. Know your happy place and have strength in knowing what takes you there. Say no to things that will make you unhappy. Don't be afraid to say no. Love yourself unconditionally and don't be afraid to let your personality shine. People will be drawn to your confidence and individuality.

Never put yourself above another. An actor is no more important than an accountant or a dustbin man and one big acting job does not make you better than other actors. Respect each other's individuality and method. Do not compete but build together and lift each other up.

No two journeys in the acting industry are the same, you just have to trust in the process. Believe this is your path, and if you must endure difficulties then it is the road which you must take to be who you are destined to be. Life has a funny way of working itself out, that's all I am saying. No matter where life takes you, I hope that someday down the road we will meet, and you will tell me all about your story. Then the first AD will call us. Make up and wardrobe will do their last-minute checks. Sound will tug and turn on our mic packs as we walk to set. The lights blind us, and we readjust to their brightness. The director finishes his coffee and tells us to take our first positions. The AD calls 'Silence on set.' The clapper board snap echoes. Camera calls 'rolling.' Director calls 'action.' And our scene will begin.

APPENDIX 1

CHARACTER QUESTIONS

PHYSICAL

Who am I?
Who am I named after? Do I like my name?
What is my gender? What do I think about my gender?
How old am I? What do I think of my age?
How does my posture express my age, health, inner feeling?
What do I look like? What do I think of it?
How tall am I? What do I think of it?
What is my weight? What do I think of it?
What is the pitch, volume, tempo, resonance or quality of my voice?
What do I think of it?
Is my articulation careless or precise?
What is my dialect or accent? What do I think of it?
What is my hair like? Colour? Style? Do I like it?
How energetic or vital am I? Do I like it?
Do I suffer from any diseases? Have I in the past?
Are my gestures compulsive or controlled?
Do I like my walk?
How do I usually sit?
How do I stand?
Do I have any items or objects with me? Why? What do they mean to me? What do I do with them?
What do I have to wear? How do I wear my clothes? How do I handle them? Do I like them?
Do I have any deformities? What do I think of them?
Do I have any mannerisms? What do I think of them?
Do I have any handicaps? What do I think of them?

SOCIAL

What do I do when I wake up in the morning?

How do I feel about my environment? Do I like it?

Am I educated? To what level? Am I intelligent?

Was I disciplined? Have I ever suffered abuse?

What was my childhood like? What are my strongest memories?

How much money do I have? How much do I want?

What is my nationality? What do I think of it?

What is my job? Do I like it? What other jobs have I had? When and why did I choose this one?

What are my political views?

Am I religious?

Who are my heroes? Who would I be if I could be anyone else? What did I like about them?

Do I like members of the opposite sex? What do I like about them?

Who were my parents? What do I like and/or dislike about them?

Do I like my family? What do I like? What do I dislike?

How has my mother influenced me?

How has my father influenced me?

Do I have brothers and sisters? What do I think about them?

What was my favourite fairy tale? Why?

Who are my friends? Who are my enemies? How can I tell if someone is a friend or an enemy?

What ideas do I like? What ideas do I dislike?

What hobbies or interests do I have?

Do I have children? Do I like them? Why? Do they like me?

What advice do I have for my children?

Am I married? Why did I marry this person?

What do I think about my lover?

What do I dislike about my lover?

How do my physical traits affect each of the social traits?

How do my social traits affect the script and my objective?

How do my social traits affect my life needs and wants?

PSYCHOLOGICAL

What choices do I have to make?
What choices do I want to make?
What makes me angry?
What relaxes me?
What are my driving ambitions, my goals?
Do I have any instincts?
Do I do things impulsively?
Do I do things tactically?
What do I worry about?
What do I want?
What do others think I want?
What do I like about myself?
Dislike about myself?
What do I need?
What am I scared of?
Why can't I get what I want?
Do other people like me?
Why do people like me?
Why do people hate me?
Do any of my psychological traits show in the way that I move?
Do any of my psychological traits show in the way that I speak?

MORALS

Are the choices I will make based upon what I can gain?
Who do I admire?
Will chasing my needs lead to a moral choice?
What is my attitude towards the choices I make?
How do I express this attitude vocally and physically?
What is my part in this story?
How do I contribute to the idea the writer is telling?
What are the words used to describe me?
What am I thinking when I enter each scene?
Where have I been prior to my scenes?

How does this affect my actions?
What am I looking for?
What are my expectations of others in the scene?

APPENDIX 2

PHOTOSHOOT CHECKLIST

- [ ] Variety of outfits
- [ ] Variety of underwear
- [ ] Variety of shoes/comfortable shoes
- [ ] Jewellery/accessories
- [ ] Makeup/nail varnish remover/moisturiser
- [ ] Powder
- [ ] Makeup wipes
- [ ] Hair spray/products/ties
- [ ] Hair electronics
- [ ] Glasses/contact lenses
- [ ] Deodorant
- [ ] Compact mirror
- [ ] Water
- [ ] Snacks
- [ ] Headphones
- [ ] Charger

APPENDIX 3

AUDITION CHECKLIST

- ☐ Learnt lines
- ☐ Research the character and story if possible?
- ☐ Researched the director/producer/production company/CD and any attached cast
- ☐ Script
- ☐ Any specified props/costume pieces, only if requested.
- ☐ Address contact and travel information
- ☐ Your agent's contact details on hand
- ☐ Photocopy of your passport
- ☐ Your sizes on hand
- ☐ Pen
- ☐ Comfortable shoes
- ☐ Makeup
- ☐ Powder
- ☐ Hairspray
- ☐ Deodorant
- ☐ Bottle of water
- ☐ Snacks
- ☐ Mints/chewing gum
- ☐ Headphones
- ☐ Phone charger
- ☐ Portable charger

APPENDIX 4

SELF TAPE CHECKLIST

- [ ] Do I know my lines?
- [ ] Do I have a reader or a play back recording of the other characters lines?
- [ ] Do I have a quiet space where I will be uninterrupted whilst recording?
- [ ] Do I have a plain and neutral backdrop?
- [ ] Is my filming equipment sufficiently charged?
- [ ] Do I have sufficient memory space for the recording?
- [ ] Is the sound recording quality good?
- [ ] Is my face well and evenly lit?
- [ ] Have I got my framing right?
- [ ] What are my edges of frame?
- [ ] Am I in focus?
- [ ] Has the scene recorded properly?
- [ ] Did I stay in character long enough at the end of my tape?
- [ ] Am I happy with my performance?
- [ ] Do I need to do less?
- [ ] Should I do another retake?
- [ ] Is a slate required at the beginning of the self tape?
- [ ] When editing have I cut any out of character moments?
- [ ] Have I properly labelled the self tape?
- [ ] In what format do I need to export the tape? Is the quality not too big/too small?
- [ ] How did the casting directors request the self tape? Direct? Website upload? Via my agent?
- [ ] Has the tape sent and been received?

APPENDIX 5

CHARACTER PREP CHECKLIST

☐ Read the script

☐ Highlight your lines in one colour

☐ Highlight your actions in another colour

☐ Take note of anything that you don't understand and research it

☐ Take note of what other people say about you and what you say about yourself.

☐ Use this information to answer the character questions in Appendix 1.

☐ Research any situations that your character experiences by asking people who have first-hand experience. Research online, watch documentaries or, where safe and appropriate to, experience it yourself

APPENDIX 6

10 STEPS TO CREATING A SUCCESSFUL PODCAST

1) Come up with a concept. It's got to be something you love and are interested in. Although podcasts are a very fast form of media in terms of turnaround time, if you want to succeed you have to be in it for the long run. It can be as specific as you like, there's an audience for everything, some obviously broader than others but the more specific, the less competition you will have. Consider relating it to your business. It will help to grow your reputation, brand and hopefully one day bring you clients and revenue.

2) Name your podcast. Spend a bit of time brainstorming. Make sure it's catchy, memorable and relates to your podcast. Most importantly check that no one else has used that name. Do this by searching your name in iTunes and checking all of the social media (Instagram, Twitter, YouTube and Facebook) platforms don't have any users with your name either.

3) Plan out your episodes for your first series. I usually plan and record ten episodes before publishing any episodes online. This means you're going to be in it for the long run, rather than letting it drop after a couple of episodes. Consistency is key! How long will they be? 10, 25, 60 minutes? It's up to you. Just make sure you have enough interesting content. Are you going to have guests? Who are they going to be? I personally think 20-25 minutes is a great length and start each episode with a question which you will discuss throughout the show. Don't be too ridged though, you're not an audiobook. Feel free to go with the flow and let the conversation take you somewhere else. Just be in control enough to bring yourself back to the point every so often.

4) Get a recording set up. Yes, you could hire a studio, but really you want recording to be as accessible as possible and in the long run it would be cheaper to buy your own equipment. Podcasts don't have to be perfect, as long as you have a quiet, peaceful

uninterrupted space throughout your recording you will be good to go.

5) Get a theme tune. Once you have figured out your branding, its usually a nice and professional touch to have some intro and outro music at the beginning and the end of your podcast. It's unlikely you will be able to use a mainstream song as they would be extremely expensive to get the rights for. Have a search on the internet for music for podcasts. Please note that you must own the rights for any audio you add on to your podcast. There will be around a £50 usage fee, depending on the artist, but it should be a one-off payment.

6) Create artwork for your podcast. This is like your album cover and will be the main thing people see when looking for a new podcast. Keep it clean, professional and eye catching. There are some brilliant designers on freelance sites who will design something for you for a very low cost. Remember to stay on brand. Make sure the colours and even the font clearly show what you are about. However, it doesn't have to be perfect just yet. Unlike your recording and theme tune, it is very easy to update your artwork on your socials and podcasting platform.

7) Edit it together! Editing a podcast together is pretty simple, it's a lot of drag and dropping. The same with adding the intro and outro music. I personally like to play with the volumes a little and cut out a few inevitable awkward pauses. In my podcast No Drama, there are three of us on one mic so every so often it needs a little tweak here and there. I edit my podcasts on a Mac using Adobe Audition which I pay about £20 for monthly, but you could use a free program on garage band or a PC equivalent. If editing is not where your skills lie then Fiverr has some great and affordable editors, although over time this could become a little costly.

8) Choose a podcasting platform. There are many great ones out there. I personally use Buzzsprout as it's super user-friendly.

It also has lots of great promoting options and helps you get your podcasts on iTunes, Spotify and Stitcher with ease. Now all you need to do is upload your edited podcast and artwork and fill in all of your info and hit the publish button. Exciting!

9) Congratulations you have a live podcast! Now you have to make sure the world can find you. Create a profile for each social media platform (Instagram, Twitter, YouTube and Facebook) using the same username. We use No Drama Podcast. Invite your friends and share exciting posts, enticing listeners to your podcast. If you are super on it, you can do this step BEFORE publishing. The more you can build up the hype and create a following, the more listens your podcast will get, meaning you could be promoted by streamer, essentially free advertising!

10) Plan out season two! By now you should know what your brand is all about. Start thinking about monetising your podcast. Ask your listeners what they do and don't like. Engage, learn from your mistakes and grow. The possibilities are endless and so is your audience.